A Catechisme
or First Instruction
and Learning
of Christian Religion
(1570)

By Alexander Nowell

Translated by Thomas Norton

A Facsimile Reproduction
with an Introduction
By Frank V. Occhiogrosso

Scholars' Facsimiles & Reprints   Delmar, New York, 1975

Published by
Scholars' Facsimiles & Reprints, Inc.,
P.O. Box 344, Delmar, New York 12054

Reproduced with permission from a copy in
The Folger Shakespeare Library
Washington, D.C.

Library of Congress Cataloging in Publication Data
Nowell, Alexander, 1507?-1602.
    A catechisme: or, First instruction and learning of Christian religion (1570)
    Reprint of the ed. printed by J. Daye, London.
    Includes bibliographical references.
    1. Church of England—Catechisms and creeds.
I. Title.
BX5139.N6   1975   238'3   74-23570
ISBN 0-8201-1143-0

142296

Introduction

Alexander Nowell

Alexander Nowell, Nowel, or Noel, dean of St. Paul's Cathedral and author of the official catechism of the Church of England, was born in Whalley, Lancashire, in 1507 or 1508.[1] He entered Brasenose College, Oxford, at the age of thirteen, and may have shared rooms there with John Foxe, the martyrologist. He was admitted B.A. in 1526 and proceeded M.A. in 1540. Having taken holy orders he was in 1543 appointed master of Westminster School,[2] where he introduced the reading of Terence. He was appointed a prebendary of Westminster in 1551, the first of many offices he would hold in the Church.

Because of his staunch Protestant views, Nowell was forced to flee to the continent during the reign of Queen Mary, residing for a time at Strasbourg and later at Frankfort. At Mary's death he returned to England and his name was included by Sir William Cecil, Queen Elizabeth's chief minister, in a list of eminent divines who were to receive preferment. He became chaplain to Edmund Grindal, afterwards Archbishop of Canterbury. In 1560 he was collated to the rectory of Saltwood with Hythe, Kent; was given a canonry at Canterbury and another at Westminster; and was finally recommended by Queen Elizabeth for election as dean of St. Paul's, which office he held from 1560 until his death more than forty years later. He was constantly appointed to preach at St. Paul's Cross, and had no small share in the restoration of the reformed religion.

On two occasions Nowell incurred the wrath of the queen. On New Year's Day, 1562, the dean presented Elizabeth with a new prayer book containing pictures of the saints and martyrs. She angrily returned the book, telling him that he had infringed her proclamation against "images, pictures and Romish relics," and she rebuked him sharply. Again, while preaching a Lenten sermon before the queen in

---

1. Here and throughout this part of the introduction I follow the article on Nowell in the *Dictionary of National Biography*, which makes use of more information than was available to the Rev. Ralph Churton when he wrote his *Life of Alexander Nowell* in 1809.

2. T.W. Baldwin, in *William Shakespeare's Small Latin and Less Greek* (Urbana, 1944), 1: 171-179, discusses Nowell as master of Westminster School and his influence upon curriculum there.

1564, he spoke slightingly of the crucifix to which Elizabeth had a special devotion. On hearing this she called aloud from her seat, "To your text, Mr. Dean—leave that; we have heard enough of that." Nowell was utterly dismayed and unable to continue his sermon.

Despite his failure to please the queen on these occasions, however, Nowell was a staunch supporter of the Anglican Church of the Elizabethan compromise. Although early on in his career he was inclined towards Calvinism in doctrine and puritanism in matters of order, he loyally complied with the ecclesiastical settlement of Elizabeth's reign. He was part of the synod which drafted the Thirty-nine Articles. He voluntarily showed his approval of certain observances, such as the keeping of holy days, that were disliked by the presbyterian party. He attempted to settle disputes within the Church over the wearing of vestments. Finally, he showed how strong was his loyalty to and belief in the principle of the Church of England in the markedly Erastian tone of some sections of his *Catechism*.

In addition to the *Catechism* (for which, see below) and his sermons, Nowell's published works include his disputation with the Catholic apologist Thomas Dorman, whose book against Bishop Jewel's *Apology* Nowell answered. The dean carried on a controversy with Dorman, with further replies in 1566 and 1567. And when Edmund Campion was in the Tower, Nowell held a disputation with the famous Jesuit, a report of which was afterwards published.

Nowell's contemporaries testified to his high standing in his own time. Among men of letters his reputation was great; many books were dedicated to him, and among other panegyrists Barnabe Googe addressed verses to him. Thomas Norton, the poet and playwright, translated his *Catechism* into English. Many testified to his piety by seeking consolation from him when dying, among them Roger Ascham, whose funeral sermon Nowell preached, and the Duke of Norfolk, who requested that the dean be present with him as the Duke awaited execution in the Tower. Nowell made significant contributions to the schools with which he was associated, and in 1595 he was created Doctor of Divinity in Oxford, with seniority over all the doctors of the university. Finally, he had the praise of Queen Elizabeth herself, who commended "his godly zeal, and special good learning, and other singular gifts and virtues."

He died on 13 February 1602, and was buried in St. Mary's Chapel, behind the high altar in St. Paul's.

Some Background to the Catechism

From the beginning the Church recognized the need to instruct its new members in the mysteries of the faith and the teachings of the

Church.[3]The Church Fathers stressed the need for such instruction, especially in three areas: the Creed, the Lord's Prayer, and the Ten Commandments. These three lessons, together with an additional one of the sacraments, became the basic four-part formula for almost all of the great catechisms written in the Reformation.

In the Middle Ages the Church made use of several agencies for the training of its youth. The first was instruction in the home. Parents had the duty to teach their children the Creed and the Lord's Prayer, and to this end a large number of tracts and books were written and widely circulated.[4]

A second method was the confessional. The Fourth Lateran Council of 1215 required all children seven years of age and older to confess at least once a year and to commune on Easter Sunday; thus the priests were able to determine both the amount and kind of instruction which the children had received at home.[5] *Catechismus* was the technical term used for the questions asked by the priests concerning the Lord's Prayer and Creed; thus the method of teaching the young by means of question and answer became part of the catechetical tradition. Special manuals were prepared to aid the clergy in their instruction of the young, among them the *Expositio symboli apostolorum* of Thomas Aquinas (1274), the *Speculum ecclesiae* of Edmund of Canterbury (1240), the *Fundamentum aeternae felicitatis* by an unknown author (c. 1470), and the *Beichtbuechlein* of John Wolff (1468).[6]Frequently the Lord's Prayer, Creed, and—especially in the fifteenth century—the Ten Commandments, were written or printed on placards and hung on the walls of schools, churches and hospitals. Towards the end of the Middle Ages knowledge of the fundamentals of religion was also spread by catechetical sermons.

A third method was religious instruction in the Latin schools, which were established in the cities after the beginning of the fourteenth century, and in the convent schools. Pupils had to memorize

---

3. Those receiving religious instruction in the early Church, prior to admission among the faithful, were called*catechumens* , from the Greek *katechoumenos* , present participle passive of*katechein* , to teach, instruct in the principles of religion.

4. A list of some of these tracts, mainly German, from the thirteenth and fourteenth centuries, is given in the first chapter of M. Reu's*Luther's Small Catechism* (Chicago, 1929). Although dealing largely with Luther's catechism, Reu's book contains much useful information on the catechetical tradition in general. See also Roland H. Bainton, *The Reformation of the Sixteenth Century* (Boston, 1952), 72-74.

5. Reu, 2.

6. Ibid.

the Lord's Prayer, Creed, Ave Maria, the grace before and after meals, the Confiteor or act of confession, and the Decalogue. But they still had as yet no real catechism. Clerics had manuals to aid them in teaching the children; but the children themselves had to wait until Martin Luther wrote a book expressly for them.[7]

The Reformation of the sixteenth century ushered in the real era of catechism writing. Perhaps because of its secure, unchallenged position on doctrine and discipline, the Church of the Middle Ages did not rely so intently on thoroughness of instruction as she suddenly felt herself compelled to do in the face of challenges from the Reformers. But even more than the defenders of the mother church, the Reformers themselves felt a great need to set down clearly and concisely a confession of their faith, a systematic exposition of doctrine, and explicit instruction in modes and forms of worship. The Reformers chose the catechism as a principle means of setting forth their differences with the Church of Rome; the Church of Rome, likewise, used the catechism as a means of showing how the Reformers were in error.

Although dozens of catechisms were written in the sixteenth and early seventeenth centuries, one quickly became the standard in each of the churches of Protestantism. In 1529 Luther's *Small Catechism* appeared; following medieval tradition it consisted of sections dealing with the Ten Commandments, Creed, and Lord's Prayer, together with two other sections devoted to the sacraments. The method is dialogue in the form of question and answer, with appropriate scriptural references supporting each answer interspersed. Calvin's *Catechism* (1542) is quite similar in content to Luther's, although the order of the first three parts is changed. The *Heidelberg Catechism* (1563), written by Zacharias Ursinus and Caspar Olevianus for the Reformed Church of the Palatinate, and which, as revised by the Synod of Dort in 1619, became the standard catechism (rather than Calvin's) in most of the Reformed churches in Europe, complicates the order of the parts still further; but the bases remain exactly the same. The first part ("Of man's misery") sets forth the two great commandments of the Law, given by Christ in the Gospel. But thereafter the familiar elements return: a second part contains the Creed, the Trinity, and the sacraments; and a third part contains the Ten Commandments and the Lord's Prayer. The Anglican catechism (i.e., Nowell's "large" *Catechism* of 1570, which this facsimile edition reproduces) also, as we shall see, contains the by now well established

---

7. Bainton, loc. cit.

four-part pattern of Decalogue, Creed, Lord's Prayer, and sacraments.[8]

Nowell's Catechism

In 1562 the Convocation of Bishops and Clergy of the Church of England advised that "there should be one perfect Catechism for the bringing up of the youth in godliness, in the schools of the whole realm."[9] There had already been several catechisms in the English Church: Cranmer had written one, based largely on Luther's *Small Catechism*, in 1547; John Poynet wrote another in 1553. But the obvious choice for the writing of this new catechism was Alexander Nowell, author of the little catechism contained in the Book of Common Prayer and published under the auspices of King Edward VI in 1549. At the time of the Convocation, in fact, Nowell was already at work on a larger version of his earlier catechism. It was approved by the bishops and clergy and subsequently also by Sir William Cecil, Elizabeth's chief minister and her closest advisor on religious matters. Nowell brought out his "large" catechism in Latin in 1570. Later in the same year a Greek translation appeared, done by Nowell's nephew, William Whitaker. Still later that year there appeared Thomas Norton's English translation with the title *A Catechism or first Instruction and Learning of Christian Religion*. Nowell later condensed this his "large" catechism somewhat, producing the so-called "middle" catechism; he abridged it still

---

8. *The Westminster Shorter Catechism*, written at the Westminster Assembly in 1648 and thereafter the standard catechism of the Presbyterian Church, differs in a number of key ways from the other Protestant catechisms. It comes out of a half-century of Puritan catechism writing, a detailed and informative history of which may be found in Alexander F. Mitchell's *Catechisms of the Second Reformation* (London, 1886).

9. See G.E. Corrie's introduction to *A Catechism, written in Latin by Alexander Nowell, together with the same catechism translated into English by Thomas Norton*, edited for the Parker Society (Cambridge, 1853), iv. The passage is also cited by Professor John R. Mulder in the chapter on Nowell's *Catechism* in his *The Temple of the Mind: Education and Literary Taste in Seventeenth Century England* (New York, 1969), 106. Professor Mulder's chapter is especially informative in showing how Nowell's *Catechism* contributed significantly to the creation of a climate of spiritual idea and expression upon which seventeenth century English poets, notably Herbert, Vaughan, and Milton, would draw heavily. See also T.W. Baldwin, *William Shakespeare's Small Latin and Less Greek* (Urbana, 1944), 1: 456-458, for the importance of Nowell's *Catechism* to Elizabethan schoolmasters.

further so that it became practically a verbatim replica of his earlier little catechism in the Prayer Book, thereby producing the so-called "small" catechism. Between 1570 and 1647 Nowell's Catechism went through forty-four editions, in Latin, English, Greek, and all bilingual combinations of these tongues. The Presbyterians replaced it with the Assembly's *Catechism* of 1648, but after the Restoration Nowell's doctrine was still in demand; his work was re-issued in 1670, 1673 and 1687.[10]On the testimony of such well known schoolmasters as Richard Mulcaster, John Brinsley and Charles Hoole, Nowell's Catechism was the standard text for the religious instruction of the young in the late Tudor and early Stuart periods.[11]

Upon examination, Nowell's *Catechism* reveals the familiar four-part organization: The First Part: Of the Law and Obedience (Decalogue); The Second Part: Of the Gospel and Faith (Creed); The Third Part; Of Prayer and Thanksgiving (Lord's Prayer); and The Fourth Part: Of Sacraments. The book also employs the question and answer technique (here, between a Master and his young Scholar) familiar from the catechetical tradition, as well as marginal references to the sources in Scripture for each item of doctrine or discipline. And the work's pedagogical function is given dignity by the early invocation of the "Scholemaister Christ" and the injunction to all to be "scholers of Christ to the end or rather without end."

Calvinist doctrine appears early in the First Part in the discussion of images in the church (referring to the Second Commandment's injunction against the making of any graven image), and their absolute prohibition is stressed. Nowell's strong Calvinistic predilections surface again in his statements on predestination and election and also in his denial of the validity of the doctrine of Transubstantiation and the Real Presence, later on in his section on the sacrament of the Lord's Supper. But there is also a strongly Erastian tone to much of the work, e.g., the section on the Fifth Commandment, where the notion of honoring one's parents is expanded to include the obeying of any magistrate or other authority figure; at that point in the *Catechism*, the church is shown to be strongly supportive of the State. Even the Tudor doctrine of Passive Obedience to one's sovereign is reinforced when the Master and Scholar discuss the heinous crime of regicide. And the Anglican Church is further strengthened—this time against dissenters and sectarians—in a discussion of the need for unity, oneness, within the Church:

---

10. Mulder, 107. For the number and dates of the editions see A.W. Pollard, G.R. Redgrave, et al., *Short-Title Catalogue of Books Printed in England, Scotland, & Ireland . . . 1475-1640* (1926) and D. Wing's addition to this work for the years 1641-1700 (New York, 1945-51).

11. Mulder, 107.

They therefore that seditiously styrre vp discorde in the Church of God, and make diuision and strife in it, and trouble it with sectes, haue all hope of safety by forgeuenesse of sinnes cut of [f] from them till they be reconciled and returne to agreement and fauour with the Church.

One of the book's closing statements is, in effect, an apology and justification for the writing of catechisms, originating out of a need for preparing children in the confession of their faith:

Parentes and scholemasters did in old time diligently instruct their children as soone as by age they were able to perceaue and vnderstâd, in the first principles of Christian Religion, that they might sucke in godlynesse almost together with the nourses milke and straight wayes after their cradell, might be nourished with the tender foode of vertue towardes that blessed lyfe. For the which purpose also little short bookes whiche we name Catechismes, were writtē: wherein the same, or very like matters, as we now are in hâd with, were intreated vppon. And after that the children seemed to be sufficiently trayned in the principles of our Religion, they brought and offered them vnto the Byshop.

This facsimile, as mentioned above, reproduces the so-called "large" *Catechism* of Alexander Nowell, in the 1570 English translation of Thomas Norton. The book is long out of print, having last been edited in the nineteenth century, and that edition is not readily obtainable today. Nowell's was the official Anglican catechism, and therefore required reading for the young, in the Elizabethan,[12] Jacobean, and Caroline eras; it was probably one of the most influential—and certainly one of the most widely read—books in English in the sixteenth and seventeenth centuries. It therefore seems reasonable to assert that any student of the history, theology, or literature of these periods would want to have at least some familiarity with the *Catechism*'s contents, and this facsimile seeks to make such familiarity possible.

* * *

Thomas Norton (1532-1584), lawyer, parliamentarian, poet, playwright, is probably best known to the student of English literature as the author, together with Thomas Sackville, of *Gorboduc* (1562), the first English tragedy and the first play in blank verse. Norton also contributed verses to Tottel's *Miscellany* and twenty-eight psalms to Sternhold and Hopkins' metrical version of

---

12. From 1570 on.

the Psalter. In addition to his translation of Nowell's *Catechism*, Norton also translated a letter of Peter Martyr's and, more significantly for the Reformation in England, the *Institutes of the Christian Religion* of John Calvin, which, like his translation of the *Catechism*, went into several editions in Norton's lifetime.

FRANK V. OCCHIOGROSSO

Drew University

A CATECHISME,

or first Instruction and Lear-
ning of Christian
Religion.

¶ *Translated out of Latine into*
Englishe.

ℐ.   𝕯.

¶ AT LONDON.
Printed by Iohn Daye
dwelling ouer Aldersgate.
¶ *Cum Priuilegio Regiæ Maiestatis*
per Decennium.
AN. 1570.

To the moſt reuerend Fathers in God, my Lordes, Mathew Archbiſhop of Canterburie and Edmond Archbiſhop of Yorke, and to the Reuerend Father in God Edwyne my lord Biſhop of London, and to all the other reuerend Fathers my Lordes the Biſhops of all the ſeuerall Dioceſes in England.

Ay it pleaſe your good Graces and Fatherhodes to permitt me, with all humilitie and reuerence to render you in this preface an accompt of my purpoſe & doing in publiſhing this Catechiſme by me tranſlated, and offred to the Chirch of England vnder protection of your names.

Wheras there was very lately a latine Catechiſme printed, wherin the ſumme of Chriſtian religion was ſett forth, in ſhort queſtions and anſwers, yet not conteyning bare and naked affirmations onely, but ſhewing alſo ſome cauſes and reaſons to the ſame annexed, and well furniſhed with places of ſcripture noted in the margine for proofe therof: in which Catechiſme there hath alſo great labor and diligence ben beſtowed about the puritie of the Latine tong, that ſuch as were ſtudious of that language, ſpecially the youth, might at once with one labor learne the truth of religion and the pureneſſe of the Latine tong together : That Catechiſme I haue thought good to tranſlate into Engliſh, as well

for the vſe of ſuch as vnderſtand no latine at all, as
alſo for their commoditie who hauing a litle ſight in
that language deſire ſome more perfection therin.
For which cauſe I haue not vſed that libertie in rendering the ſenſe at large, which the order of tranſlati-
on doth permitt vnto me, but haue willingly for the
benefit of the meaner learned, tyed my ſelfe very
much to obſeruing of the wordes themſelues, but ſo
yet that I had alway regard to the naturall propertie
and eaſineſſe of our natiue tong.

This booke as it will be profitable to ſuch as do
vnderſtand Engliſh onely, ſo will it bring double
profit to thoſe, who being ſomwhat ſkilled in the
latine tong and deſiring more ſkill, will compare the
Latine booke with the Engliſh, whereby they may
at once learne, as I ſayd, the truth of religion, and the
puritie of the Latin tong. And leaſt the reader deſirous to compare any the partes or ſentences of the
Latine and Engliſh bookes, might be hindered, I
haue procured that the Engliſh print anſwereth the
Latine, page for page throughout the whole bokes,
ſo that any ſentence may at the firſt eaſily be found
in both the bookes. This exerciſe in my opinion is
moſt mete for the vſe of ſuch eccleſiaſticall miniſters
and ſtudious youth as haue not yet the perfect
knowledge either of religion or of the Latin ſpeche,
who by experience may finde (as I thinke) more
profit hereby then they would ſuppoſe vpon the firſt
view. Neither is this conference of tranſlations, by
them who be very well learned iudged vnprofitable
for ſuch as are competently learned.

The booke hath alſo one further vſe of very good
exerciſe for thoſe that deſire to ſee more at large
how the doctrine herein taught is confirmed by the

word

word of God the only rule of true religion, that is, if
such as shall reade it to learne truth, but specially ecclesiasticall ministers whose charge is to teach truth,
shal resort to the places of scripture noted in the margine & rede them in the Bible at large & then marke
how eche thing here affirmed is there well confirmed, and how the doctrine here deliuered is not
onely in all partes fully approued by Gods holy
word, but also for the most part vttered in the very
wordes of the text, so farr as may be with respect of
purenesse of the Latin phrase. By which meane they
shall also be occasioned to be better acquainted with
the scriptures them selues and with the true and naturall vnderstanding of them . And therin be it remembred that the last numbres in the quotations
shewing the diuisions within the chapiters, are gathered according to the great Bible last printed. This
exercise who so shall assay shall finde it of maruellous
great profit, both for conceyuing truth to the satiffi-
ing of conscience, and for deliuering truth to the
discharge of dutie.

It may perhappes be maruelled of some, why
throughout the booke, as well in the Latin as in this
translated, the Master asketh, the Scholar answereth,
and euer the declaration of the matter is put in the
scholars mouth, so as some may muse why the scholar may seme to be made wiser then the maister. This
obiection hath easy answer, & such answer as it hath
I thought mete to disclose . It may not be thought
that the maister here enquireth of the scholar as de-
sirous to learne of him, nor that the scholar enfor-
meth the maister as presuming to teach him. But the
maister opposeth the scholar to see how he hath profited, & the scholar rendereth to the maister to geue

A.iij.   accompt

accompt of his memory and diligence. And that it may appere that this order of opposing by the maister and rendering by the scholar, for good reason might seme to the author more conuenient than the other forme which some other writers of catechismes haue vsed, that is, of enquiring by the scholar, and teaching by the maister, (without preiudice alway or condemning the other) it may be remembred that the end and purpose of Catechisme is in good and naturall order fitly applied to serue the good vse of Confirmation by the bishop, at which time the bishop which confirmeth, doth not teach but examine, and in his whole maner of opposing vseth such forme as here in like sort the *Catechumenus* or childe is prepared vnto. Which is also not done without example, for the same maner is in the short Catechisme now vsed in the church of England at Confirmation.

Now surely there are no greater meanes of auauncing true religion, and rooting out of errors, than these two, that is to say, Catechisme or good instruction of youth, and good information of ecclesiasticall ministers in sound truth & the proues therof, howsoeuer perhappes they may lacke some full furniture of other learninges. And therewith for my part I haue long thought it a much better way toward remouing of heresies & superstitions (whereof Rome hath brought vs & left vs plentie) to deale first with plaine setting out of truth as not in controuersie, without dealing at the beginning with the strife of confutation. For so both discretion and charitie in the teacher is easilier kept, and truth once being settled, error will fall of it selfe, so that he which hath once thus with conference of Gods word
conceiued

conceiued a certaine and ſtayed iudgement of
truth , ſhall either wonder how abſurde errors
haue ben recciued, or ſhall with leſſe perill heare
them talked of.

Theſe thinges all conſidered,and how this boke
ſerueth to all theſe good endes, and therewithall remembred how it hath pleaſed almighty God of his
great goodneſſe and loue, and to the ſingular benefit of this his Chirch of England,vnder the Queenes
moſt excellent maieſtie the moſt honorable inſtru-
ment of auauncing his religion and glory in her do-
minions and of bringing truth and peace to the conſciences of her ſubicétes, to ordeine your graces and
fatherhodes the chefe paſtors and gouerners of his
flocke for doctrine and all eccleſiaſticall duties : the
firſt author of this boke in Latine had very good
reaſon to offer his worke vnto you, that as the people of Gods flock in England are vnder your charge,
ſo they might receiue ſo great a benefit as this is vnder your name, and thereby you our gouerners on
the one part might be the rather moued to further
ſo good intention , & we all vnder your gouernance
on the other part be made more redy to receiue it
with better aſſurance of good alowance,& to thanke
God the geuer of all good thinges, and guyder of all
good doinges and purpoſes,and(as mete is)that we
and our poſteritie , ſo long as an Engliſh childe or o-
ther ſhall in this catechiſme learne Chriſtianitie,may
kepe in thankfull remembrahce the happineſſe of
theſe good times , the bleſſed memorie of her maieſtie , and the good names of you Gods good miniſters now chefe paſtors of this his flocke, in whoſe
time(to your and our comfortable conſideration be
itſpoken) God hath ſo liberally ſpred among vs the

light

light of his gospell, and (praised be he, and happy be ye therfore) hath made you his faithfull dispensers of so great a grace.

The same reasons that so moued the first author, haue also moued me to offer my translation· vnto you , comprising herein as patrones all the fathers and lordes of the Clergie, but specially and by name your graces my Lordes the Archbishops , to whose prouinces the whole realme perteineth, and your fatherhode my Lord of London to whose Diocese London a light to the rest of England belongeth, and to whom my selfe dwelling within your charge do owe particular dutie.

This my intent and labor being to do good to as many and largely as I possibly could, if I shall vnderstand to be with the Reders taken in good part and vsed to their benefit, (as the rather by your good meanes, and names it may be) I shall thinke my trauail very well bestowed , holding my selfe in the meane time contented with the conscience of a good meaning bent to do good so farre as my skill and power would extend. The successe herof I committ to God, the iudgement I submitt to you, for whom and whose zele I prayse God, and pray to him for your preseruation to the benefit of his Chirch.

(∴)

Your most humble.   T. Norton.

The Maiſter.   The Scholar.

The Maiſters dutie.

Oraſinuch as the maiſter ought to be to his ſcholars a ſecond parent and father, not of theyr bodyes but of their myndes, I ſee it belógeth to the order of my dutie, my dere child, not ſo much to inſtruct thee ciuilly in learnyng and good maners, as to furniſh thy mynde, and that in thy tender yeres, with good opinions and true Religion . 'For this age of childhode ought no leſſe, yea alſo much more, to be trayned with good leſſons to godlineſſe, than with good artes to humanitie. Wherfore I thought mete to examine thee by certaine ſhort queſtions, that I may ſurely know whether thou haue well beſtowed thy ſtudie and labor therin or no.

Godlineſſe in childhode.

Deut.4.b.9.10.6.b.12.13. Pſal.78.a.3.4.6. Mat.19.b.13. 2.Tim.3.b.14.

Scholar. And J for my part, right worſhypfull Maiſter, ſhall willingly anſwere your demaundes, ſo far as J haue ben able with witt to conceiue or kepe in memorie, and can at this preſent call to mynde and remember, what J haue heard you teach me out of the holy Scriptures.

Maiſter. Goe to therfore, and tell me what Religion it is that thou profeſſeſt.

Schol. The Religion that J profeſſe, right worſhypfull maiſter, is the ſame wherof the Lord Chriſt is the author and teacher, and which is

Chriſtian Religion.

B.j.   ther=

Christian, na=
med of Christ.

* Act.11.b.26.

therfore properly and truely called the Christian
Religion , lyke as the professers therof are also
named Christians.

Ma. Doest thou then acknowledge thy selfe to be a
folower of Christian godlynesse and Religion, and a
scholar of our Lord and scholemaster Christ?

* Rom.10.b.9.10.

* Psal.1.g 73.c.12.
John.3.c.18.b.36.

Sch. I do so acknowledge in dede, and do vn=
faynedly & freely professe it . Yea I do settle ther=
in the summe of all * my felicitie, as in that which
is the chiefest good that can come to man, & such
as without it our state should be farre more mise=
rable than the state of any brute creatures.

Ma. Well then, I would haue the substance and na=
ture of Christian Religion and godlynesse, the name
wherof is most honorable and holy, to be briefly ex=
pressed with some definition of it.

The definition.

* Deut.4.a.1.2.g 10.
b.17.
Psal.119.a.4.
Mat.4.b.10.
John.4.a.24.

Schol. Christian Religion is the * true and godly
worshyppyng of God, and kepyng of hys com=
mandementes.

Ma. Of whom doest thou think it is to be learned?

* Psal.1.a.7.g 73. a.
3. g 119.cc12.
John.1.g.39.
2.Tim.3.b.15.

Sch. Of none other surely but of the heauenly
* word of God him selfe , which he hath left vnto
vs written in the holy Scriptures.

Ma. What writynges be those which thou callest
the word of God and the holy Scriptures?

* Exod.17.b.15.16.
Deut.4.a.11
Luk.16.g.29.31. & 24
a.27.b.44.
2.Pet.1.b.20.

* John.1.a.3.g.9. & 8.
b.12.
Heb.1.a.1.2.

* Mat.28.b.18.
John.30.f.21.
Act.2.a.4. Eph.3.a.5.

* Esa.40.b.8.
Mat.5.c.18.
Luk.16.b.17.

Sch. None other but those that haue bene pu=
blished, first by Moses & the holy Prophetes the
frendes of almighty God , by the instinct of the
Holy ghost in the old Testament, and afterward
more playnly in the new Testamēt by our * Lord
Jesus Christ the sonne of God, and by his holy
Apostles inspired with the spirite of God, & haue
ben * preserued vnto our tyme whole and vncor=
rupted.

M 4.

Ma.   Why was it Gods will so to open vnto vs his word in writyng?

Sch.   Bicauſe we of our ſelues (ſuch is the * darkneſſe of our hartes) are not able to vnder-ſtand the will of almighty God , in the ˙know-ledge of whom & in obedience toward him true godlyneſſe conſiſteth, God hauyng pitie vpon vs hath * opened & clerely ſet it out vnto vs, and the ſame ſo clerely ſet out he hath left in the booke of the two ˙Teſtamentes, which are called the holy * Scriptures, to the end that we ſhould not be vncertainely ˙caried hether and thether, but that by hys heauenly doctrine there ſhould be made vs as it were a certaine entrie into heauen.

Ma.   Why doeſt thou call Gods word a Teſtament?

Sch.   Bicauſe it is euident that in conceiuyng of Religion it is the chiefe point to vnderſtand what is the * will of the euerliuing God . And ſithe by the name of Teſtament is ſignified not onely a will, but alſo a ˙laſt & vnchangeable will, we are hereby admoniſhed that in Religion we * folow nothyng, nor ſeke for any thyng, further than we are therin taught by God, but that as there is one onely true God , ſo there be but one godly worſhyppyng & pure Religion of one onely God. Otherwiſe we ſhould daily ˙forge our ſelues new fayned Religions, and euery nation, euery citie, & euery man , would haue his owne ſeuerall Reli-gion, yea we ſhould in our doinges follow for our guide , not Religion and true godlyneſſe the be-gynnyng and foundation of vertues , but ſuper-ſtition à deceitful ſhadow of godlineſſe. Which is moſt plaine to ſee , by the ſundry and innumera-ble not religions but worſe than dotyng ſuperſti-

B.ij.   tions

*John.1.a.1.
1.Cor.2.c.11.
Ephe.4.c.17.18.

*Mat.7.c.21.& 13.
b.50.
Heb.10.g.36.
1.John.2.c.17.

*Sap.9.b.16.17.
Act.26.b.18.
1.Pet.1.b.9.

*Gal.4.c.24?
Heb.3.b.6.& 9.b.15.

*Mar.16.f.16.
2.Tim.3.b.16.

*Mat.11.c.29.
Mat.11˙c.24.

*Mat.7.d.21.& 13.
b.50.

*Gal.3.d.17.19.

*Deut.4.a.2.5.b.32.
& 13.b.19.

*Mat.15.a.9.c.6.d.9.

tions of the 'old Gentile nations, who otherwise in worldly matters were very wise men.

Ma. Doest thou then affirme that all thinges necessarie to godlynesse and saluation are conteyned in the written worde of God?

Sch. 'Pea, for it were a point of intolerable vngodlinesse & madnesse to thinke, either that God hath left an vnperfect doctrine, or that men were able to make that perfect which God left vnperfect. Therfore the Lord hath most straightly forbidden men, that they neither *adde any thing to, nor take any thing from his word, nor turne any way from it either to the right hand or to the left.

Ma. If this be true that thou sayest, to what purpose then are so many things so oft in Councels and ecclesiasticall assemblies decreed, and by learned men taught in preaching, or left in writing?

Sch. All these thinges serue either to expounding of darke places of the word of God, and to take away controuersies that rise among men, or to the orderly stablishyng of the outward gouernance of the Church, and not to make new articles of Religion. 'For all thyngs necessarie to saluation, that is to say, how godlynesse, holynesse, and Religion, are to be purely and vncorruptedly yelded to God: what obedience is to be geuen to God, by which alone the order of a godly lyfe is to be framed: what affiance we ought to put in God: how God is to be called vpon, and all good thinges to be imputed to him: what forme is to be kept in celebrating the diuine misteries: all these thinges, I say, are to be learned of the word of God, without the knowlege whereof, all these thinges are either vtterly vnknowen

O3

oʒ most abſurdly done, ſo as it were farre bet=
ter that they were not done at all, as the Loʒd
himſelfe witneſſeth, that * ignoʒance of the ſcrip=
tures is the mother of all erroʒs, and he himſelfe
in his teaching doth commonly allege the * wʒit=
ten woʒd of God, & to it he ſendeth vs to learne
of it. Foʒ this cauſe therefoʒe, in old tymes alſo,
the woʒd of * God was openly read in chirches,
and the helpe of expounders vſed when they
might haue them, as appeareth by the hiſtoʒies
of the chirch. And the Loʒd himſelfe, immediat=
ly befoʒe his aſcending to heauen, gaue principal=
ly in charge to his Apoſtles whom he had choſen,
* that they ſhould inſtruct all men thʒoughout
the woʒld with his woʒd. And Paul folowing
his example, * oʒdeined that ſome ſhould be ap=
pointed in euery chirch to teache the people, foʒ
that he well knew that faith and all thinges per=
teining to godlineſſe do hang vpon the reading
* and hearing of the woʒd of God, and that ther=
foʒe * Apoſtles, teachers, Pʒophetes and expoun=
ders are moſt neceſſary in the chirch of God.

Ma. Doeſt thou then thinke that we are bound to
heare ſuch teachers and expounders?

Sch. Euen as the Loʒd himſelf if he were pʒeſent,
ſo farre as they teach onely thoſe thinges which
they haue receaued of the Loʒd. Which himſelfe
witneſſeth, ſaying, * he that heareth you heareth
me, he that deſpiſeth you deſpiſeth me. Yea and
moʒeouer to theſe pʒeachers of his woʒd * he hath
geuen the power to binde and looſe, that whoſe
ſinnes ſoeuer they by the woʒd of God ſhall par=
don oʒ deteine in earth, the ſame ſhall be pardo=
ned oʒ deteyned in heauen.

            B.iij.   *Ma.*

Ma. Is it enough to heare them once treate of religion?

Sch. * We ought to be the scholers of Christ to the end or rather without end. It is not therfore enough for a man to beginne vnlesse he continue. And such is our * dulnesse and forgetfulnesse, that we must oft be taught and put in remembrance, oft pricked forward and as it were pulled by the eare. For thinges but once done or seldome heard are wont lightly to slippe out of mynde. And for this cause (as is aforesayd) * euery sabbat day (as appeareth by the ecclesiasticall histories) the people assembling together, the word of God was openly read, and the expounders thereof if any were present were heard. Which custome is also at this day receaued in our churches, by the ordinance of the Apostles, and so of God himselfe.

Ma. Doest thou then thinke that the word of God is to be read in a strange tong and such as the people vnderstandeth not?

Sch. That were grossly to mock God & his people, & shamelessly to abuse them both. For whereas God commaundeth that his word be plainely read to * yong and old, men and women, namely to the entent that all may vnderstand and learne to feare the Lord their God, as he himself in his owne word expressly witnesseth: it were a very mockery, that the word of God which is appointed by God himselfe to teach his people, should be read to the people in a tong vnknowen to them, and whereof they can learne nothing. Also Saint Paul doth treate of this matter * and thereupon concludeth that the vnlearned people

Marginal notes:
* 1 Math. 10. c. 22. & 24. b. 13.
Luc. e. g. 61.
Rom. 11. c. 22.
1. Cor. 9. b. 24.
2. Tim. 3. b. 14.

* Judic. 3. a. 2.
PSL 106. a. 4. b. 14.
Hierom. 2. g. 31.
Luc. 24. b. 25.

* Act. 13. c. 15. b. 27. & 15. b. 21.

* Deut. 4. b. 10.
Deut. 31. c. 11. 12. 13.
Josue. 8. g. 11.
2. Paral. 34. g. 30.

* 1. Cor. 14. b. 16.

people can not aunſwere *Amen* to the thankeſge-
geuing which they vnderſtand not, but that the
reders and the hearers ſhould be * ſtrangers the   • ₁.Cₒᵣ. ₁₄.ₐ. ₁₆.
one to the other, if any thing be ſpoken in the
congregation, that is not vnderſtoode of them
that be preſent:* and that he had rather to ſpeake   • ₂. ₁₉.
in the church of God fiue wordes vnderſtoode,
then ten thouſand wordes not vnderſtoode.

Ma. Shall we then haue ſufficiently diſcharged our
duties, if we ſo endeuor our ſelues that we heare
and vnderſtand the word of God?

Sch. No. For we muſt not onely heare and vn-
derſtād the word of God, but alſo * with ſtedfaſt   • pſal. ₁.ₐ.₆. ₁₉.ₐ.
aſſent of mynde embrace it as the truth of God   ₈.₉.₁₀.
deſcended from heauen, and hartly loue it,* yeld   Mar.₁₆.ₐ.₁₆
our ſelues to it deſirous and apt to learne, and to   act.₁₃.g. ₄₈
frame our myndes to obey it, that being once   • Deut.₃₁.ₐ.₁₂.
planted in our hartes, it may take deepe rootes   ₂.Paral.₃₄.g.₃₈
therein and bring forth the fruites of a godly life   Luc.₁₁.ₐ. ₂₈
ordered according to the rule thereof, that ſo it   Job.₇.ₐ.₂₄.
may turne to our ſaluation as it is ordeined.* It   Jacob.₁.ₐ.₂₂. ₂₃.
is therefore certayne that we muſt with all our   • Deut.₁₇.ₐ.₁₉.
trauaile endeuor ,that in reading it , in ſtudying   Joſue.₁.ₐ. ₈
vpon it, and in hearing it both priuately and pu-   pſal.₁. ₐ.₂.
blikely, we may profit :but profit in any wiſe we
can not, if it be ſet forth to vs in a tong that we
know not.

Ma. But ſhall we atteine to ſuch perfection as thou
ſpeakeſt of, by onely reading the word of God and
diligently hearing it, and the teachers of it?

Sch. Foraſmuch as it is the wiſdome of God,
men ſhould vainely labour in either teaching or
learning it, vnleſſe God would vouchſafe with   • Deut.₂₉.ₐ.₄.
the * teaching of his ſpirit to inſtruct our hartes,   Luc.₂₄.ₐ.₂₅.₂₇.₄₅.
               B.iiij.   as   ₄₁.₄₆.
   act.₁₆.ₐ.₁₄.
   ₂.Cor.₄.ₐ.ₐ.

• 1.Cor.3.b. 7.

as Paul teacheth,* that in vayne is the planting and the watering vnlesse God geue the encrease. Therefore, that we may atteine the wisdome of

• Psal. 36.c.11.& 119.
b.33.34.35.

God hidden in his word, we must* with feruent prayer craue of God that with his spirit he

• Mat.6.g.13
Joan.1.a.5.
1.Cor.2.b.14.

lighten our myndes being darkened * with extreame darknesse. For him the Lord hath promised to vs to be our* teacher sent from heauen that

• Joan.16.b. 13.

shall guide vs into all truth.

Ma. Into what chiefe partes doest thou deuide all

¶The diuision of the word of God.

this word of God.

Sch. Into the Law and the Gospell.

Ma. How be these two knowen th'one frō the other.

Sch. The law setteth out our duties, both of godlinesse toward God, that is, the true wor-

• Mat.22.b.36.
Mar.12.c.30.
1.Joan.3.b. 23.

shipping of God, and of *charitie toward our neighbour, and seuerely requireth and exacteth

•Le.:6.toto.
Deut. 4. b. 32.&
33. toto.
Joan.14.b.15. & 21.23.

* our precise obedience, and to the obedient promiseth euerlasting life, but to the disobedient pronounceth threatninges and paynes, yea and

• Mar.1.b.15. & 16.
b. 16.
Luc.1.f.73. & 24.g.47.
Joan.1.b.17.
Act.2.f.38. & 3.f.38.
Rom.1.b.16.
Gal.3.b. 13.

eternall death.The Gospell * conteineth the promises of God,& to the offenders of the law,so that they repent them of their offence, it promiseth that God wil be mercifull through faith in Christ.

• The summe of all that hath bene sayd.

M. Hetherto then thou hast declared that the*word of God doth teach vs his will,and conteineth all thinges needefull to saluation, and that we ought earnestly to studie vpon it, and diligently to heare the teachers and expounders of it, but aboue all thinges that we must by prayer obteine vs a teacher from heauen, and what is the word of God, and of what partes it consisteth.

Sch. It is true.

Ma. Sithe then Christian Religion floweth out of Gods

Gods word as out of a spring hed: as thou haſt before done with Gods word, ſo now diuide me alſo Religion it ſelfe which is to be drawen out of Gods word, into her parts & members, that we may plainly determine wherunto eche part ought to be applied, and as it were to certaine markes to be directed.

Sch. As of the word of God, ſo of Religion alſo there are principally two partes.* Obedience, which the Law the perfect rule of righteouſneſſe commaundeth: and Faith,* which the Goſpell, that embraceth the promiſes concerning the mercy of God, requireth).

Ma. It ſemeth yet that there are either moe, or other partes of Religion, for ſometime in diuiding it the holy ſcriptures do vſe other names.

Sch. That is true. For ſometime they diuide whole Religion into Faith* & Charitie, & ſometyme into * Repentaunce & Faith. For ſometime for Obediēce they ſet*Charitie, which by the law is required to be perfect toward God and men: and ſometime becauſe we performe neither obedience * nor charity ſuch as we ought, they put in place thereof * Repentance moſt neceſſary for ſinners to the obteining of the mercy of God. Some which like to haue moe parts, do ſet forth firſt out of the law,* the knowledge of our due duty, and damnation by the law for forſaking and reiecting our duty: ſecondly out of the Goſpell, the * knowledge and affiance of our deliuerance: thirdly, * prayer and crauing of the mercy and helpe of God: fourthly,*thankſgeuing for deliuerance and other benefites of God. But howſoeuer they differ in names, they be the ſame thinges, and to thoſe two principall partes Obe-

C.j.   Dience

(margin notes)
Religion diuided.

* 2 Cor.16.a.3.b.14. Deut.11.b.16. Ioan.14.b.15.c.22. 23.24.

* Mar.1.b.15.g 15. b.15.16. Rom.1.a.7.b.16.g 3. c.22.g 4.tota.

* Gal.1.a.6. 1.Ioan.3.b.29.
* Mar.1.b.15.

* Math.22.B.37.39. Mar.12.c.30.31.ggo

*Pſal.14.a.2. Rom.3.b.9.
* Math.4.c.17. Mar.1.b.15. Act.2.c.38.

* Rom.3.c.20.g 7.b.7.

* Rom.3.c.24. Galat.1.c.16.

* Pſal.32.a.5.6. Rom.10.c.12.13.

* Col.1.c.11.g.2.b.14. Ephe.1.a.4. 6.30. Phil.4.a.6. Coloſ.3.c.17.

dience and Faith, in which is conteined all the summe and substance of our Religion, all the rest are referred. For wheras many do adde as parts, inuocation and thankesgeuing, and the diuine misteries most nerely conioyned to the same, which are commōly called Sacraments, these in very deede are compriſed within those two former partes. For no man can truely performe the duty toward God either of affiance or of obedience, which will not when any necessity distreſſeth hym, flee to God and accompt all thinges to come from him, and when occasion and tyme ſerueth rightly vſe his holy misteries.

Ma. I agree with thee that all may be drawen to theſe two partes, if a man will preciſely and ſome-what narrowly treate of them. But foraſmuch as the moſt preciſe maner of diuiding is not to be required of children, I had rather that ſomwhat in plainer ſort thou diuide Religion into moe parts, that the whole mater may be made the clearer. Therfore let vs han-dle theſe thinges more groſly, ſo it be more openly.

Sch. Where you like best to deale with me in plainer ſort, I may conueniently of two partes make fower, and diuide whole Religion into Obedience, Faith, Inuocation, and Sacramentes.

Ma. Go to then. Sithe I deſire to haue this treating of Religion to be as plaine as may be, let vs kepe this order, firſt to enquire of Obedience, which the Law requireth: ſecondly of Faith, which loketh to and embraceth the promiſes of the Goſpell: thirdly of Inuocation and thankeſgeuing, which two are moſt nerely ioyned together: fourthly and laſty, of the Sacramentes and myſteries of God.

Sch. And I, worshipfull maister, shall willingly
accor-

according to my slender capacitie answere your
questions, as I am taught by the holy scriptures.

The first part.   Of the Law and Obedience.

Ma. Forasmuch as * our Obedience, whereof we
haue first to speake, is to be tryed by the rule of the
law of God, it is necessary that we first search out the
whole substance & nature of the Law : which being
found and knowen, it can not be vnknowen, what
and of what sort our obedience ought to be. Therefore beginne to tell what thou thinkest of the Law.

Sch. I thinke that the law of God is the * full,
and in all pointes perfect, rule of the righteousnesse that is required of man, which * commaundeth those things that are to be done, and forbiddeth the contraries. In this law God hath * restrained all thinges to his owne will and iudgement, so as no godlinesse toward him, nor duti-
fulnesse toward men, can be allowed of him, but
that onely which doth in all thinges agree with
the streightnesse of this rule. Vainely therefore
do mortall men inuent to themselues formes of
* godlinesse and dutie after their owne fansie.
For God hath set forth to vs his law * written in
two Tables as a most sure rule both of our worshipping of God and * of our duties to men,
and therewith also hath declared that there is
nothing on earth more pleasant * and acceptable
to him than our obedience.

Ma. Whereof treateth the first Table?

Sch. It treateth of our * Godlinesse toward
God, and conteineth the first fower commaundementes of the law.

Ma. Whereof treateth the second?

        C.ij.   **Sch.**

Marginal references:

* Lam. 16. a. 3. b. 14.
Deut. 10. b. 12. and 32. tota.
Psal. 119. a. 4.
Luc. 10. c. 25.
Iean. 14. b. 15. c. 21. 23. 24.
Iacob. 2. b. 10.

* Deut. 4. a. 1. & 5. a. per to. & 12. d. 4.
Psal. 19. b. 6. 7.

* Exo. 20. tota. &
Deut. 5.
Esa. 30. d. 21.

* Deut. 6. c. 17. 18. & b. 13.
Rom. 12. d. 2.
Eph. 5. c. 17. & 6. b. 7.
Colos. 1. b. 9.

* 1. Reg. 15. a. 22.
Esa. 26. c. 13.
Mat. 15. a. 3. 9.

* Matth. 22. b. 36. 40.
1. Joh. 3. b. 23.

* Exo. 31. b. 18. and 34. b. 28. 29.
Deu. 4. b. 13.

* Deu. 5. b. 31. and 30. c. 11. and 11. b. 26.
Math. 19. c. 16.
1. Joh. 5. b. 24.

* Deut. 6. b. 5.
Mat. 22. b. 36.

*Mat.22.b.39.
Rom.13.c.2.p.
Gal.5.c.14.*

*Exo.34.b.28.
Deut.4.b.13.*

Sch. Of the duties of * mutuall Charitie or loue among men, which conteineth sixe commande- mentes. And so in à summe, * ten commande- mentes make vp the whole law. For which cause the law is called the Ten commandementes.

Ma. Rehearse me the first commandement of the first table.

*Exo.20.a.1.2.3.
Deu.5.a.6.7.
Psal.81.b.9.p.
Mich.6.b.4.*

Sch. God spake thus.* *Heare O Israell: I am the Lord thy God which haue brought thee out of the land of Egipt, out of the house of bondage . Thou shalt haue none other Gods before me.*

Ma. Why doth God first speake somewhat of him- selfe and of his benefite?

*Exod.16.a.both.
Deut.6.b.6.*

Sch. He had principally care that the * estimati- on of the lawes ordeined by him, should not be shortly abated by contempt. And therefore that they might haue the greater authoritie, he vseth this as it were an entrie, *I am the Lord thy God.*

*Deut.10.c.18.
Psal.135.a.5 136.a.1.
Esa.1.c.13.& 43.a.1.
Malec.1.b.10.
1.Tim.6.c.14.15.16.*

In which wordes he teacheth that he is * our maker, lord and sauiour, and the author of all good. And so with good right by his dignitie of à Lawmaker, he chalengeth to himselfe the au- thoritie of commanding: and by his goodnesse, he procureth fauour to his law: and by them both to- gether, burdeneth vs with necessitie to obey it,

Malac.1.b.p.6.

vnlesse we will be both * rebelles against him that is most mighty, and vnthankefull toward him that is most bountifull.

Ma. But wheras he speaketh of Israel by name, and maketh expressly mention of breaking the yoke of the bondage of Egypt: doth not this belong one- ly to the people of Israel?

Apoc.12.g 14.

Sch. God in deede rescued the Israelites by his seruant Moses from bodily * bondage, but he hath

hath deliuered all them that be his, by his sonne
Iesus Christ from the spirituall * thraldome of
sinne, and the tyrannie of the Deuill, wherin els
they had lien pressed and oppressed. This kinde
of deliuerance perteineth indifferently to * all
men, which put their trust in God their deliuer-
rer, & do * to their power obey his lawes. Which
if they do not, he doth by this rehearsall of his
most great benefit pronounce that they shalbe
* gilty of most great vnthankfulnesse. For let e-
uery man imagine the * Deuill that hellish Pha-
rao ready to oppresse him, and how *sinne is that
most foule mier wherein he most filthily wallo-
weth, let him set before the eyes of his minde hell
*the most wretched Egyptian bondage, and then
shall he easily perceaue that this freedome wherof I speake is the thing that he ought principally
* to desire, as the thing of most great importance
to him, whereof yet he shall be most vnworthy,
vnlesse he honor the * author of his deliuerance
withall seruice and obedience.

Ma. Say on.

Sch. After that he hath thus stablished the authoritie of his law, now foloweth the commandement. *Thou shalt haue none other Gods before me.*

Ma. Tell me what this meaneth.

Sch. This commaundement condemneth & forbiddeth idolatry, * which God throughly hateth.

Ma. What is idolatry, or to haue strange Gods?

Sch. It is in the place of the one only *true God
which hath openly and manifestly shewed and
disclosed himselfe vnto vs in the holy scriptures,
to set other persons or thinges, and of them * to
frame and make to our selues as it were cer-

C.iij.   tayne

Marginal references:
* Iob.5.b.14.16.
Iohn.8.b.20.
Col.1.b.11.
Ioh.2.b.14.15.
Acti.10.c.35.

* 1.Ioh.3.c.22.

* Iob.5.f.11.
1.Ioh.5.b.2.

* Psal.15.b.13.14.&
103.a.1.
Iere.2.b.6.

* Luc.13.b.16.
2.Cor.2.b.10.
1.Pet.5.b.8.

* Psal.40.a.2.
Esa.19.A.3.
2.Pe.2.b.20.22.
Apoc.16.c.13.

* Mat.13.f.40.
Luc.16.c.23.
2.Pet.1.a.4.

* Mat.16.b.26.
Act.26.b.18.
Rom.16.c.20.

* Esa.17.c.10.
Ioh.14.b.15.
Rom.6.c.17.
1.Cor.6.b.19.

* Leuit.26.a.1.a.13.
Deut.12.a.3.
Iudi.10.b.6.c.14.

* Deut.6.a.4.5.7.
Mat.11.c.28.29.30.

* Esa.44.c.17.
Deut.5.a.7.c.8.12.19.

tayne Gods, to worship them as Gods, and to set and repose our trust in them. For God commaundeth vs to * acknowledge him alone for our onely God , that is, that of those thinges that wholy belong to his maiestie and * which we owe to him alone, we transferre not any part be it neuer so litle to any other, but that to him alone and entirely we geue his whole honor and seruice, whereof to yeld any whit to any other were a most hainous offence.

Ma. What be the thinges that we properly owe to God alone, wherein thou sayest that his proper and peculiar worshipping consisteth?

Sch. Innumerable are the thinges that we owe to God , but they all may be well reduced to foure chiefe pointes.

Ma. Which be they?

Sch. That we geue vnto his Maiestie * the soueraigne honor, and to his goodnesse the greatest * loue & assiance, that we flee to him * and craue his helpe, that with thankefulnesse we yelde * as due to him our selues and al that we haue. These thinges are to be geuen, as to none other, so to him alone, if we desire to haue him alone our * God, and to be his peculiar people.

Ma. What meane those last wordes, *before me or in my sight.*

Sch. That we can not once so much as tend to reuolting from God, but that God is * witnesse of it: for there is nothing so close nor so secret that can be hidde from him. Moreouer he thereby declareth that he requireth not onely the * honor of open confession, but also inward and sincere godlinesse of hart, for that he is the vnderstander and iudge

iudge of ſecret thoughtes.

Ma. Well then, let this be enough ſayd of the firſt commaundement. Now let vs goe on to the ſecond.

Sch. *Thou ſhalt not make to thy ſelfe any grauen image, nor the likenes of any thing that is in heauen aboue or in the earth beneath, nor in the water vnder the earth : thou ſhalt not bow downe to them, nor worſhip them. For I the Lord thy God, am a * ielious God, & viſite the ſinnes of the Fathers vpon the children vnto the third & fowerth generation of them that hate me, and ſhew mercy vnto thouſandes in them that loue me, & kepe my commandementes.*

Ma. What is the meaning of theſe wordes.

Sch. As in the firſt commandement he commandeth that himſelf alone be honored and worſhipped, ſo in this commandement he reſtraineth vs from all ſuperſtition, and from all wrongfull and bodily inuentions, foraſmuch as the worſhipping of him ought to be * ſpirituall and pure: and chiefly he * frayeth vs from the moſt groſſe fault of outward idolatrie.

Ma. It may ſeeme then that this law wholly condemneth the artes of painting, and portraiture, ſo that it is not lawfull to haue any images made at all.

Sch. Not ſo. But he firſt forbiddeth vs to make any images to * expreſſe or counterfait God, or to worſhip him withall, and ſecondly he * chargeth vs not to worſhip the images themſelues.

Ma. Why is it not lawfull to expreſſe God with a bodily and viſible forme?

Sch. Becauſe there can be no likeneſſe or agreeing betwene God which * is a ſpirit, eternall, vnmeaſurable, infinite, incomprehenſible, ſeuered from all mortall compoſition, and a fraile, bodily, ſilly, ſpiritleſſe, and * vaine ſhape. Therefore they do most iniuriously abate the maiestie of the most good and most great God, when they goe about in such sort to make resemblance of him.

Ma. Haue not they then sayd well, which affirme that images are vnlearned mens bookes?

Sch. I know not what maner of bookes they be. But surely, concerning God, they can teach vs nothing but errors.

Ma. What maner of worshipping is that which is here condemned?

Sch. When we intending to pray do * turne our selues to portraitures or images, when we do fall downe and kneele before them, with vncouering our heades or with other signes shewing any honor vnto them, as if God were represented vnto vs by them. Briefly we are in this law forbidden, that we neither seeke nor worship God in images: or, which is all one, that we worship not the images themselues in honor of God, nor in any wise by idolatrie or superstition abuse them with iniurie to his maiestie. Otherwise the lawfull vse * of making portraitures, and of painting, is not forbidden.

Ma. By this that thou tellest me it may easily be gathered that it is very perilous to set any images or pictures in churches which are * properly appointed for the onely worshipping of God.

Sch. That that is true, we haue had already to much experience by the decay in a maner of whole religion.

Ma. Yet there remayneth a certaine as it were addition or appendant of this law.

Sch. For I (saith he) I the Lord your God * am a ielous

God,

God, and viſit the ſinnes of the fathers vpon the children
vnto the third & fourth generation of them that hate me.

Ma. To what end, or wherfore were theſe thinges
ſpoken?

Sch. Theſe ſerue to thys end, to ſtabliſh and confirme thys law by adding as it were a certaine
ſpeciall decree. For in naming him ſelfe our Lord
& our God, he doth by two reaſons, that is, in re-
ſpect * of his authoritie, & of his bountifulneſſe,
vrge vs to obey him in all thinges. And by this
word *Ialouſie, he declareth that he can abide no
partener or egall.

Ma. What is the reaſon of this ialouſie that thou
ſpeakeſt of?

Sch. A moſt iuſt reaſon. For ſith that to vs which
haue *nothing deſerued, onely of his own infinite
goodneſſe, he hath geuen him ſelfe, by moſt good
right it is that he will haue vs to be * wholly
altogether & entirely his owne. For this is that
*bond as it were of a holy mariage, wherein to
God the faithfull huſband our ſoules as chaſte
ſpouſes are coupled. Whoſe chaſtitie ſtandeth
in this, to be dedicate to God alone, and to cleaue
wholy to him, like as on the other ſide our ſoules
are ſayd to be * defiled with adulterie, when they
ſwarue from God to idolatrie or ſuperſtition.
And how much more hartily the huſband loueth
his wife, and the chaſter he is him ſelfe, ſo much is
he more greuouſly diſpleaſed with his wife when
ſhe breaketh her fayth.

Ma. Goe on.

Sch. Now to the entent to ſhew more behement-
ly how he hateth idolatrie, & with greater feare

D.j.   **to**

to restraine vs from offending therin, he threate-
neth that he will take vengeance, not onely of
them that shall so offend, but also * of their children and posteritie.

Ma. But how doth this agree with the righteousnesse of God, that any one should be punished for
an others offence?

Sch. The very state of mankinde doth sufficiently assoile this question. * For by nature we are all
subiect to damnation, in which state if God do
leaue vs, we haue no cause to complaine of him.
And as toward the godly he sheweth his loue &
mercie, * in defending & cherishing their posteritie with geuing them their preseruation which
he ought them not, so toward the vngodly he
executeth his vengeance in * withholding that
his goodnesse from their children, and yet in the
meane time he doeth them no wrong, in that he
geueth them not the grace which * he oweth
them not, but as he found them, so leaueth them
to their owne disposition and nature.

Ma. Go forward to the rest.

Sch. That he should not seeme to enforce vs
with onely threateninges, now foloweth the
other part, wherin God with gentle and liberall
promising, entreateth and allureth vs to obey
him. For he promiseth that * he will shew most
great mercifulnesse, both toward all them selues
that loue him and obey his commandementes,
and also toward their posteritie.

Ma. By what reason doest thou thinke this to be
righteous?

Sch. Some reason it is, bicause of the godly education.

cation*wherin godly parents do so instruct their children that they commonly vse to succede them as their heires in the true feare & loue of God. Also * nature it selfe draweth vs to a good will toward our frendes children. But the surest reason is that God so promiseth , * which neither can swarue from righteousnesse , nor at any time breake his promise.

Ma. But it appeareth that this is not continually certaine,and euer falleth so. For sometime godly parentes begette *vngodly children, and such as goe out of kinde from their parentes goodnesse, whom God(notwithstanding this promise) hath greuously punished.

Sch. This in deede can not be denied. For as God,when he will, *sheweth himselfe mercifull to the children of the wicked, so is he by no such necessity bounden to the children of the godly, but that he *is at libertie to reiect such of them as he will. But therin he alway vseth such moderation that the truth of his promise euer remaineth stedfast.

Ma. Where afore we speaking of reuenging, he nameth but three or foure generations at the most, why doth he here, in speaking of mercie, conteine a thousand?

Sch. To shew, that he is much more inclined to *mercifulnesse and to liberalitie, than he is to seueritie,like as also in an other place he professeth that he is very slow to wrath and most redy to forgeue.

Ma. By all this that thou hast sayd , I see thou vnderstandest, that God made speciall prouision, that the worshipping of him, which ought to be spirituall and most pure, should not be defiled with any grosse idolatrie or superstition.

Sch. Yea, he most earnestly prouided for it. For he hath, not onely plainely and largely reckoning vp all formes of images, decreed it in a maner in the first part of his law as a thing that principally concerneth his maiestie, but also hath confirmed this law with terrible threatenings to the offender, and on the other side offering most great rewardes to the obseruer of it. So that it may well seeme more then wonderfull, that this commaundement either was not vnderstoode as beyng obscure, or not espied as lying hid in the multitude, or not regarded as light or of small charge, yea that it hath lien as it were wholly neglected of all men, as if it had bene no commandement, with no threatenings, no promises adioyned vnto it.

Ma. It is true as thou sayest. But now rehearse me the third commandement.

Sch. *Thou shalt not take the name of thy Lord God in vaine. For the Lord will not holde him giltlesse that taketh his name in vaine.*

Ma. Tell me, what is it to take the name of God in vaine?

Sch. To abuse it, either with forswearing, or with swearing rashly, vnaduisedly, and without necessitie, or with once naming it without a weightie cause. For sithe the maiestie of Gods name is most holy, we ought by all meanes to beware, that we seeme not either to despise it our selues, or to geue other any occasion to despise it: yea

yea & so to see that we neuer once ˙vtter þ name
of God without most great reuerence, that it
may euer appeare honozable & glozious both to
our selues & to al other. Foz it is not lawful once
˙ to thinke, much lesse to speake of God and of his
wozkes, otherwise than to his honoz. Briefly
whosoeuer vseth the name of God otherwise
than foz most weighty causes and foz most holy
matters, abuseth it.

Ma. What thinkest thou then, of them that blas-
pheme God, and of sorcerers and such other kindes
of vngodly men ?

Sch. If they do great iniurie to God, which ˙vse
his name onely of a certaine lewd custome and
vntemperate redinesse of speche, much moze do
they make themselues gilty of a most hainous
and outragious offence which abuse the name
of God, ˙in banninges, in cursinges, in enchant-
mentes, in forespeakinges, oz in any other maner
of superstition.

Ma. Is there any lawfull vsing of the name of God
in swearing?

Sch. Yea forsooth. When ˙an othe is taken foz
a iust cause, either to affirme a truth, specially if
the magistrate require oz command it, oz foz any
other matter of great impoztance, wherein we
are either to mainteine vnuiolate the honoz of
God, oz to pzeserue mutuall agreement and charitie among men.

Ma. May we therefore lawfully, whensoeuer we
say truth, vse an othe with it?

Sch. I haue already said that this is not lawfull,
foz so the estimation and reuerence of the name

of God should be abated, and should become of
no price, and contemned as common. But when
in a * weighty matter, the truth should otherwise not be beleued, we may lawfully confirme
it with an oth.

Ma. What followeth next?

Sch. *For the Lord will not hold him giltlesse that taketh*
his name in vaine.

Ma. Sithe God doth in other places pronounce
that he will punish generally * all the breakers of his
law, why doth he here particularly threaten them
that abuse his name?

Sch. Hys meaning was to shew how highly he
esteemeth the * glory of his name, to the end that
seing punishment ready for vs, we should so
much the more hedefully beware of prophanely
abusing it.

Ma. Doest thou thinke it lawfull to sweare by the
names of saintes, or by the names of other men or
creatures?

Sch. No . For sithe a lawfull othe is nothing els
but the swearers religious affirming that he calleth and vseth God * the knower and iudge of all
thinges for witnesse that he sweareth a true othe,
and that he calleth vpon and wisheth the same
God to be the punisher and reuenger of his lying
and offence if he sweare falsly: it were a most
hainous sinne, to part or communicate among
other persons or creatures this honor of Gods
wisedome and maiestie which is his owne proper and * peculiar honor.

Ma. Now remayneth the fourth Commaundement, which is the last Commandement of the first
Table.   Sch,

Sch. *Remember that thou* * *keepe holy the Sabbat day.*
Sixe dayes shalt thou labour, and do all that thou hast to do.
But the seuenth day is the Sabbat of the Lord thy God . In
it thou shalt do no maner of worke, thou & thy sonne & thy
daughter, thy manseruant, & thy maidseruant, thy cattell,
and the stranger that is within thy gates . For in sixe dayes
the Lord * *made heauen and earth, the sea, and all that in*
them is, and rested the seuenth day . Wherefore the Lorde
blessed the seuenth day, and hallowed it.

Ma. What meaneth thys worde Sabbat.

Sch. Sabbat by interpretation signifieth * Reſt.
That day, for that it is * appointed onely for the
worſhipping God, the godly muſt lay aſide all
worldly buſineſſe, that they may the more diligently intend to Religion and godlineſſe.

Ma. Why hath God ſet herein before vs an example
of him ſelfe, for vs to followe?

Sch. Becauſe notable and noble * examples do
more throughly ſtirre vp & ſharpen mens minds.
For ſeruantes do willingly follow their maiſter,
and children their parent . And nothing is more
to be deſired of men, than to frame themſelues to
the * example and imitation of God.

Ma. Sayeſt thou then that we muſt euery ſeuenth
day abſteine from all labor?

Sch. Thys Commandement hath a double conſideration . For in ſo much as it conteineth a ceremonie and requireth onely outward reſt, it
*belonged peculiarly to the Jewes, and hath not
the force of a continuing and eternall law . But
now by the *comming of Chriſt, as the other ſha-
dowes of Jewiſh ceremonies are abrogate, ſo is
thys law alſo in thys behalfe abridged.

           D.iiij.   Ma.

Ma. What then, beside the ceremonie, is there remayning, wherunto we are still perpetually bound?

Sch. Thys law was ordeined for three causes: fyrst, to stablishe and mainteine an * ecclesiasticall Discipline and a certaine order of the Christian common weale: secondly, to prouide for the * state of seruauntes that it be made tolerable: thirdly, to expresse a certaine forme and * figure of the spirituall rest.

Ma. What is that ecclesiasticall Discipline that thou speakest of?

Sch. That the people assemble together, to*heare the doctrine of Christ, to yelde * confession of their fayth, to * make openly publike prayers to God, to celebrate and reteine the ˙ memorie of Gods workes and benefites, and to vse the ˙ misteries that he hath left vs.

Ma. Shall it be enough to haue done these euery seuenth day?

Sch. These thinges in deede euery man priuatly ought to ˙ record and thinke vpon euery day, but for our negligence and weakenesse sake, one certayne speciall day is by publike order appointed for this matter.

Ma. Why was there in this commandement prouision made for releuing of seruantes?

Sch. It was reason that they which be * vnder other mens power should haue some time to rest from labour. For els their state should be too greuous and to hard to beare. And surely meete it was, that seruantes should together ˙ with vs sometime serue him that is the common maister of them and vs, yea and father too, sithe he hath

by

by Chzist adopted them to himself as well as vs.
It is also pzofitable foz the maisters themselues,
that seruantes should sometime rest betwene
their wozkinges, that after respiting their wozke
a while, they may returne moze fresh and lusty
to it agayne.

Ma. Now remaineth for thee to tell of the Spirituall rest.

Sch. That is when resting from wozldly busi-
nesse, and from our owne wozkes and studies,
and as it were hauing a certaine holy vacation,
we yeld our selues wholly to Gods gouernance,
that he may do his wozkes in vs : and when (as
the scripture termeth it) * we crucifie our flesh,
we bzidle the frowald desires and motions of
our hart, restrayning our owne nature, that we
may obey the will of God. Foz so shall we most
aptly reduce and bzing the figure and image of
eternall rest to the very thing and truth it selfe.

Ma. May we then cast away this care on the other
dayes?

Sch. No. Foz when we haue once begonne, we
must goe fozward to the end, * thzoughout the
whole race of our life. And the number of * seuen,
fozasmuch as in the scripture it signifieth perfection, putteth vs in remembzance that we ought
with all our fozce and endeuoz continually to la-
boz and * trauaile toward perfection : and yet
therwithall is it shewed vs that so long as we
liue in this wozld, we are * farre from the perfection and full atteining of this spirituall Rest, and
that here is geuen vs but a certaine taste of that
Rest, which we shall enioy * perfectly, fully, and

most

most blessedly in the kingdome of God.

Ma. Hetherto thou hast wel rehearsed me the lawes of the first Table, wherin the true worshipping of God which is the fountaine of all good thinges, is briefely comprehended. Now therefore I would haue thee tell me what be the duties of our Charitie and Loue toward men, which duties do spring and are drawen out of the same fountaine, and which are conteined in the second Table.

*Exo.20.b.12.
Deu.5.b.16.
Mat.15.a.4.
Eph.6.b.2.4.*

Sch. The second Table beginneth thus. * *Honor thy Father and thy mother: that thy dayes may be long in the land which the Lord thy God geueth thee.*

Ma. What is ment in this place, by this word Honor?

*Prou.1.a.8.
Mat.15.b.10.19.
Colos.3.c.20.
1.Tim.5.a.4.
Heb.12.c.9.*

Sch. The Honor of parentes conteineth loue, * feare, and reuerence, and consisteth as in the proper worke and dutie of it, in obeying them, in sauing, helping, and defending them, and also finding & releuing them if euer they be in neede.

Ma. Doth the law extend onely to parentes by nature?

*Deu.17.c.10.
Rom.13.a.1.
*Lut.10.f.16.
1.Tim.5.a.1.
*Prou.5.c.13.
Iob.2.b.31.
*Leu.19.f.32.
Pron.19.b.10.*

Sch. Although the very wordes seeme to expresse no more: yet we must vnderstand that all those, to whom any authoritie is geuen, as * magistrates, *ministers of y̆ chirch, *scholemasters, finally all they that haue any ornament either of * reuerend age, or of witte, wisdome, or learning, worship or wealthy state, or otherwise be our superiors, are conteined vnder the name of fathers: bicause the authoritie both of them and of fathers come out of one fountaine.

Ma. Out of what fountaine?

*Deu.17.c.10.
Cit.5.a.1.
1.Pet.2.b.13.*

Sch. The * holy decree of the lawes of God, by
which

which they are become worſhipfull & honozable,
as well as naturall parentes. Foz from thence
they all, whether they be parentes, pzinces, magiſtrates oz other ſuperiozs whatſoeuer they be,
haue all their power and authozitie, bicauſe by
theſe it hath pleaſed God to rule and gouerne
the wozld.

Ma. What is ment by this that he calleth magiſtrates and other ſuperiors by the name of parentes?

Sch. To teach vs, that they are geuen vs of God
both foz owne and * publike benefit, and alſo by
example of that authozitie which of all other is
naturally* leaſt grudged at, to traine and enure
the minde of man which of it ſelfe *is puſſed with
pzide and loth to be vnder others commaundement, to the dutie and obedience toward magiſtrates. Foz by the name of parentes, we are
charged not onely to yeld & obey to magiſtrates,
but alſo to honoz and loue them. And likewiſe
on the other part ſuperiozs are taught ſo to gouerne their inferiozs, as a iuſt parent vſeth to
rule ouer good childzen.

Ma. What meaneth that promiſe which is added to
the commandement?

Sch. That they ſhall * enioy long life, and ſhall
long continue in ſure and ſtedfaſt poſſeſſion of
wealth, that geue iuſt and due honoz to their parentes and magiſtrates.

Ma. But this promiſe ſeemeth to belong peculiarly to ſuch Iewes as be kinde to their parentes.

Sch. It is no doubt, that, that which is by name
ſpoken of the land of * Chanaan, perteineth onely to the Iewes. But fozaſmuch as God is

         C.ij.   *Lozd

Gen.1.a.1.
Psal.74.a.1.g 115.b.16
Deut.4.a.6 &c.

*Lord of the whole world, what place soeuer he geueth vs to dwell in, the same he promiseth and assureth vs in this law that we shall keepe still in our possession.

Ma. But why doth God recon for a benefit, long continued age in such a miserable and wicked life?

1.Reg.11.a.1.
2Chal.15.a.1.2.3.
Iere.14.b.5.
Deut.5.b.19.

Sch. Because when he releueth the miseries*and calamities of them that be his , or preserueth them in so many periles that beset them round about, and calleth them backe from vices and sinnes, he sheweth to them à fatherly minde and good will, as to his children.

Ma. Doth it follow on the contrarie side, that God hateth them whose life is taken away quickly or before their ordinarie race of yeares expired, or that be distressed with miseries and aduersities of this world?

Iob.1.d.11.g 5.a.17.
Prou.3.b.12.
Heb.5.b.10.11.

Sch. Nothing lesse. But rather, the *deerelier that any man is beloued of God, he is commonly the more burdened with aduersities, or is wont the soner to remoue out of this life, as he were deliuered and let by God out of prison.

Ma. Doth not this in the meane tyme seeme to abate the truth and credit of Gods promise?

Deut.28.a.1.2.
Col.1.a.19.20.
Iohn.22.a.4.5.

Sch. No. For when God doth promise vs worldly good thinges, he alwayes addeth this exception either expressely vttered * or secretly implied, that is, that the same be not vnprofitable, or hurtfull to our soules. For it were against order and reason, * if chiefe regard should not be had of

Mat.5.b.25.g 18.a.8
1.Reg.7.a.14.15.
2.Cor.6.b.2.

the soule, that we may so either attaine or * lacke worldly commodities, as we may with blessednesse enioy eternall life for euer.

Ma.

Ma. What shall we then say of them that be disobedient to parentes or magistrates, or do missuse them, yea or kill them?

Sch. Commonly all such do either * continue a most vile and miserable life, oʒ lose it most shamefully beyng taken out of it with vntimely and cruell death, oʒ infamous execution. And not onely in this life, but also in the * woʒld to come, they shall foʒ euer suffer the euerlasting punishment of their vngodlinesse. Foʒ if we be foʒbidden by the commandement of God, as here next foloweth, to hurt any men be they neuer so much estranged frõ vs, yea * euen our aduersaries and deadly enemies, much moʒe to kill them, surely it is easy to perceiue, how much we ought to foʒbeare and beware of all doing of any iniurie to our parentes of whom we receiue our life, inheritance, libertie, and countrey. And since it is notably well sayd by the wise men in olde tyme, that naturall dutie may be bʒoken with a looke, and that it is a most hainous wickednesse once to offend his parentes with woʒd oʒ speech: what punishment can be found sharpe enough foʒ him that shall offer death to his parent, foʒ whome himselfe ought to haue bene content to die by the law of God and man, if nede so required?

Ma. But it is much more hainous for a man to offend or kill the parent of his countrey than his owne parent.

Sch. Yea surely. Foʒ if it be foʒ euery pʒiuate man, a hainous offence to offend his pʒiuate parentes, and parricide to kill them: what shall we say of them that haue conspired and boʒne wicked

E.iij.   ked

ked armour, against the common weale, against their countrey the most auncient, sacred, and common mother of vs all, which ought to be dearer vnto vs than our selues, and for whom no honest man will sticke to die to do it good, and against the prince the father of the countrey it selfe and parent of the common weale: yea and to imagine the ouerthrow, death, and destruction of them, whom it is hie treason once to forsake or shrinke from? So outragious à thing can in no wise be expressed with fit name.

Ma. Now rehearse the sixth Commandement.

Sch. *Thou shalt not kill.*

Exo.20.b.13.
Mat.1.c.21.
Iac.2.b.11.

Ma. Shall we sufficiently fulfill this law, if we keepe our handes cleane from slaughter and bloud?

Sch. God made his law not onely for outward workes, but also and chiefly for the * affections of the hart. For * anger and hatred and euery desire to hurt is before God adiudged manslaughter. Therefore these also God by this law forbiddeth vs.

Deu.30.b.6.
Gal.24.b.4.
Mat.6.d.4.
Heb.5.c.12.
Mat.5.c.21.22.23.
Gal.5.b.20.
1.Joh.2.b.15.

Ma. Shall we then fully satisfie the law, if we hate no man?

Sch. God in condemning hatred, requireth loue *toward all men, euen our enemies, yea so farre as to wish health, safetie, and all good thinges to them that wishe vs euill, and do beare vs a hatefull and cruell mynde, and as much as in vs lieth to do them good.

Mat.5.c.39.44.45.
Luc.6.b.27.
Rom.12.b.18.

Ma. What is the seuenth Commaundement.

Sch. *Thou shalt not commit adulterie.*

Exo.20.b.14.
Deu.5.b.18.
Mat.19.c.18.

Ma. What doest thou thinke to be conteined therin?

Sch. By this commaundement is forbidden all

kinde

kinde of filthy and wandering luſt, and all vncleaneſſe that riſeth of ſuch luſt, as fondneſſe in
handling, * vnchaſtneſſe of ſpech, and all wan-
tonneſſe of countenance and geſture, all outward ſhew of vnchaſtitie whatſoeuer it be. And
not onely filthineſſe of wordes & vncleaneſſe of
doinges is forbidden by God, but alſo foraſmuch
as both our bodies and our ſoules are * the temples of the holy ghoſt, that honeſtie may be kept
vndefiled in them both, ſhamefaſtneſſe and chaſtitie is commanded, that neither our bodies be
defiled with vncleaneſſe of luſt, nor our myndes
with vnhoneſt thoughtes * or deſires, but be alway preſerued chaſt and pure.

*Rom.11.D.19.
1.Cor.6.B.9.
Iac.2.b.14.

*1.Cor.3.B.d.17.&
6.D.15.19.
2.Cor.6.B.16.

*Iob.31.A.9.
Prou.6.d.25.
Mat.5.B.27.28.

Ma. Goe on to the reſt.

Sch. The eight Commandement is : * *Thou ſhalt
not ſteale*. By which Commandement are condemned not onely thoſe theftes which are puni-
ſhed by mennes lawes, but alſo all fraudes * and
deceiuinges. But none doth offend more hai-
nouſly againſt this law, than they that are wont
by meane of truſt to beguile them toward whom
they pretend frendſhip. For they that breake
faith, labour to ouerthrow the common ſuccour
of all men. We are therfore commanded that we
deceaue no man, that we vndermine no man,
that we ſuffer not our ſelues to be allured with
vantage or gaine of bying or ſelling to do any
wrong, that in trading of bying or ſelling we
ſeeke not wealth vniuſtly, nor make our profit
by vntrue and vneuen *meaſures and waightes,
nor encreaſe our riches with ſale of ſlight and deceitfull ware.

*Exo.20.B.15.
Mat.19.c.18.
1.Cor.6.b.B.9.10.

*1.Theſ.4.b.6.
Eſa.5.b.1.&c.

*Prou.11.a.1.&20.
b.10.d.11.

E.iiij.　Ma.

Ma. Thinkest thou there is any more to be sayd of this Commandement?

Sch. Yea forsooth. For not onely outward theftes & fraudes are forbidden, and we are commanded to vse bargaining without guile and deceites, and to do all thinges els without suttle vndermining, but also we are charged to be altogether so minded, that though we were sure to escape vnpunished and vnespied, yet we would of our selues forbeare from wrong. For that which is wrong before man to do, is euill before God to haue will to do. Therefore all counsells and deuises, and specially * the very desire to make our gaine of others losse is forbidden by this law. Finally we are by this law commanded to endeuor all the wayes we may that euery man may most spedily come to his owne and safely keepe that which he possesseth.

Ma. What is the ninth commaundement?

Sch. *Thou shalt * beare no false witnesse against thy neighbour.*

Ma. What is the meaning of this commandement?

Sch. That we* breake not our othe or fayth. And in thys lawe we are forbidden not onely open and manifest periuries, but also wholly all lying, sclanders, * backbitinges, and euill speakinges, wherby our neighbour may take losse or harme, or lose his good name and estimation. For one example conteineth a generall doctrine. Yea and we ought neither our selues at any time to speake any false or vntrue thing, nor with our wordes, writing, silence, presence, or secrete assent in holding our peace, once allowe the same in other.

But

* Psal. 62. b. 10.
Zach. 8. c. 17.
Mich. 2. a. 12.
Rom. 10. g. 33.

* Exo. 20. c. 16.
Deut. 5. c. 20.
Mat. 19. c. 18.

* Exo. 23. a. 1.
Leuit. 19. c. 11. 12.
Deu. 19. b. 18. 19.
Mat. 19. c. 18.

* Psal. 15. a. 4.
Soph. 3. c. 13.
Iam. 4. d. 14.

But we ought alway to be *louers & foliowers of simple truth, euer to rest vpon truth, to bring forth all thynges diligently into the light of truth as place, time, or necessitie shall require, finally euer redily to take vpon vs the defence of truth, and by all meanes to mainteine and vphold it.

Ma. For satisfying of this lawe, is it not enough to bridle our tong and penne?

Sch. By the same reason that I haue before said, when he forbiddeth euill speaking, he therewith also forbiddeth sinister*suspicions and wrongfull misdeminges. For this Lawmaker hath euer chiefe respect to the affections of the hart. Thys law therefore forbiddeth vs to be inclined so much as to thinke euill of our neighbours, much lesse to *defame them. Yea it commaundeth vs to be of such gentle sinceritie and indifferencie toward them, as to endeuor, so farre as truth may suffer, to thinke well of them, & to our vttermost power to preserue their estimation vntouched.

Ma. What is the reason why the Lorde in hys lawe doth terme the corrupt affections of the hart, by the names of the most hainous offences? For he comprehendeth wrath & hatred vnder the name of manslaughter : all wantonnesse, and vncleane thoughtes, vnder the name of adulterie : and vniust coueting, vnder the name of theft.

Sch. Least we (as the nature of man is) should winke at the vngodly* affections of the hart, as thinges of small weight, therefore the Lorde setteth them out by their true names, according as he measureth them by the rule of hys owne righteousnesse. For, our Sauiour the best interpreter of hys fathers meaning, doth so expound the
F.j.   same:

* Mat.5.v.21.22.&.27.
b.19.
1.John.3.v.15.
same : *who so (sayth he) is angry with hys bro-
ther, he is a manslayer : who so lusteth after a
woman, he hath committed adulterie.*

Ma. But whereas onely vices and sinnes are forbidden in these commaundementes, why doest thou in
expounding them, say that the contrary vertues are
also commaunded therein? For thou sayest that in
forbidding of adulterie, chastitie is enioyned, and in
forbidding manslaughter & theft, most entier good
will and liberalitie is commaunded. And so of
the rest.

* Mat.22.v.39.
Rom.13.v.8.9.
Gal.5.v.14.
* Psal.37.v.27.
Sch. Because the same our Sauiour doth so expound it, which setteth the summe of the lawe,
not in absteyning onely from iniurie and euill
doing, but in * loue and charitie, like as the king-
ly Prophet had also before taught, saying: Depart from euill, and do good.

Ma. Now remayneth the last commaundement.

* Exo.20.v.17.
Mich.2.v.2.
Rom.7.v.7.
1.Cor.10.b.6.
Sch. *Thou shalt not couet * thy neighbours house. Thou
shalt not couet thy neighbours wife, nor his seruant, nor his
maide, nor his oxe, nor his asse, nor any thing that is his.*

Ma. Seing that, as thou hast oft sayd already, the
whole law is spirituall, and ordeined not onely to
restraine outward euill doinges, but also to bridle the
inward affections of the hart: what is there herein
commaunded more that was before omitted?

* Eccle.1.b.16.
Rom.13.b.14.
Gal.5.b.16.
Sch. God hath before forbidden euill doinges,
and corrupt affections of the minde : But now
he requireth of vs a *most precise purenesse, that
we suffer not any desire be it neuer so light, nor
any thought be it neuer so small, in any wise
swaruing from right, once to crepe into our hart.

Ma. How then? doest thou say, that vnaduised and
sodeine desires, and short thoughtes that come vpon
the

the very godly, are sinnes , although they striue a-
gainst such rather than yelde to them?

Sch. Surely it is playne that all corrupt
* thoughtes, although our consent be not added
to them, do procede of our corrupted nature. And
it is no dout that sodeine desires that tempt the
hartes of men , although they preuaile not so
farre as to winne a stedfast assent of minde and
allowance, are in this commandement condemned by God as sinnes . For it is meete that euen
in our * very hartes and mindes shoulde shine
before God,their most perfect purenesse & cleannesse . For no innocencie and righteousnesse * but
the most perfect can please hym,whereof he hath
also set before vs this his law a most perfect rule.

Ma. Hetherto thou hast shortly and plainly opened the lawe of the ten commaundementes.But can
not all these thinges that thou hast seuerally and particularly declared, be in fewe wordes gathered as it
were into one summe?

Sch. Why not? seing that Christ our heauenly
scholemaister hath comprised the whole pith and
substance of the lawe in a summe & short abridgement, in thys maner, saying : * *Thou shalt loue the
Lord thy God with all thy hart , with all thy soule, with all
thy minde,and with all thy strength . And this is the greatest commaundement in the law . And the second is like
vnto this : Thou shalt loue thy neighbour as thy selfe . For
in these two commaundementes are conteined the whole
Law, and the Prophetes.*

Ma. What maner of loue of God, doest thou take
to be here required?

Sch. Such as is mete for God, that is, that we
acknowledge * hym both for our most mighty

F.ij.   Lord

• Sir.6).v.16.
Mic.b.c.
1.Tim.i.a.i.

• Deut.10.c.12.
Psal.16.a.7.
1.Cor.10.g.jb

• Deu.6.c.17.
Rom.12.a.1.

• Psa.7.b.17.c.15.a.1.
c.31.a.1.c.118.b.

Lord, and our most louing *father and most mer-cifull Sauiour. wherefore to thys loue is to be adioyned, both *reuerence to hys maiestie, & obe-dience to *his will, and *affiance in his goodnesse.

Ma. What is meant, by *all the hart, all the soule, all the strength?*

• Deu.30.b.6.
Jos.23.c.11.
Mat.10.b.37.
Luc.14.f.26.

Sch. Such feruencie and such vnfainednesse of loue, that there be no roome for any * thoughtes, for any desires, for any meaninges or doinges that disagree with the loue of God. Deare (as one sayth) are our parentes, deare are our chil-

• Job.14.b.17.c.21.37.
c.31.b.10.

dren, our kinsfolkes, our frendes, and dearer yet is our countrey: but all the deare * loues of them all, entier zeale toward God, and the most perfect loue of hym not onely conteineth, but also much and farre surmounteth, for whom, what good man will sticke to dye? For euery godly man loueth God not onely more dearely than all hys, but also more dearely than him selfe.

Ma. Now, what sayest thou of the loue of our Neighbour?

• 1.Cor.13.a.30
Eph.5.c.29.
Philip.2.a.1b

Sch. Christes will was that there should be most streight bondes of loue among hys Christians. And as we be by nature most * inclined to the loue of our selues, so can there not be deuised a plainer, nor shorter, nor more pithy, nor more in-different rule of brotherly loue, than that which the Lorde hath gathered out of our owne nature and set before vs, that is, that euery man should beare to hys neighbour the same good will that he beareth to him selfe. whereof it foloweth,

• Mat.7.b.12.c.22.b.39.
Luc.6.b.31.
Rom.13.c.9.10.

that we should * not do any thing to our neigh-bour, nor say nor thinke any thing of him, which we would not haue other to do to our selues, or

to

to say oʒ thinke of our selues. Within the com-
passe of which onely law, which is in deede as it
were the soule of all other lawes, if we could be
holden, surely there were no neede of so many
barres of lawes, as men do dayly deuise to hold
men in from doing wʒong one to an other, & to
mainteine ciuile societie, & all welnere in vaine
if among men this one law be not regarded.

Ma. How farre extendeth the name of Neighbour?

Sch. The name of Neighbour conteineth, not
onely those that be of our kinne and alliance, oʒ
frends, oʒ such as be knit to vs in any ciuile bond
of loue, but also those whom we * know not, yea
and our enemies.

Ma. Why? what haue those to do with vs?

Sch. Surely they are knit to vs with the same
bond, wherewith God hath coupled together all
mankind; which bond his will is to haue inuiolable and *stedfast, and therfoʒe it can not be taken away by any mans frowardnesse, hatred, oʒ
malice. Foʒ though any man hate vs, yet that
notwithstanding he remaineth still our neighbour, and so must alway be accompted, bicause
the same oʒder by which this felowship and conioyning among men is knitt together, ought alway to remaine stedfast and inuiolable. And
hereby it may be easily perceaued why the holy
scripture hath apointed Charitie oʒ * loue to be
one of the pʒincipall partes of Religion.

Ma. But what meaneth that addition in the end,
that therein are conteined the whole law and the
Prophetes.

Sch. Because in very deede the summe of them
all belongeth thereunto. Foʒ all the warninges,,

commandementes, exhortations, promises, and threateninges, which the law it selfe and the prophetes and Apostles do euery where vse, are directed to nothing els but to the end of this law as it were to a marke. And * all things in the holy scriptures are so applied to charitie, that they seeme as it were to leade vs by the hand vnto it.

Mat.-.b.12.
Luc.o.b.31.
Rom.13.c.8.10.
Gal.5.b.14.
1.Tim.1.b.5.

Ma. Now I would haue thee to tell me, what law that is that thou speakest of. Whether is it the same that we call the law of nature, or some other besides it?

Sch. J remember maister, that J haue long agoe learned this of you, that is, that the law, as the hyest reason, was by God graffed in the nature of man, while mans nature was yet * sound and vncorrupted, being created after the image of God, and so this law is in deede and is called the lawe of nature. But since the nature of man became stained with sinne, although the * mindes of wise men haue bene in some sort lightened with the brightnesse of this naturall light, yet in the most part of men this light is so put out, that scarce any sparcles thereof are to be seene: and in many mens mindes is deepely graffed * a sharpe hatred of God & men, against the ordinances of God & his commandements written in this law, which command most harty loue to God & men. And hereof commeth so great vngodlinesse toward God, and so deadly crueltie toward men.

Gen.1.b.26.27.31.
Eph.4.f.24.
Colos.3.b.10.

Luc.1.g.79.
Act.14.d.17.& 17.f.27.
Rom.2.d.19.

Math.24.f.9.10.b.12.
Joh.17.c.14.
3.Tim.3.d.2.

Ma. How commeth it to passe that God would haue these commandementes written in Tables?

Sch. J will tell you. * The image of God in man, is since the fall of Adam by originall sinne and by euill custome so darkened, and naturall iudgement

Luc.1.g.79.
1.Cor.2.b.14.
Eph.4.d.17.18.

ment

ment so corrupted, that man doth not sufficiently vnderstand what difference is betwene honest
and dishonest, right and wrong. Mercifull God
therefore, minding to renue the same image in
vs, hath by his law written in tables, set forth
the rule of * perfect righteousnesse, and that so
liuely and fully that God requireth no more of
vs but to follow the same rule. For he accepteth
none other sacrifice but * obedience, and therfore
he hateth all whatsoeuer it be that we admitte in
religion or in the case of worshipping God without the warrant of his prescribed ordinance.

Ma. But where in this law there are no commandementes set out of euery mans priuate vocation, how
can this be a perfect rule of life?

Sch. Though here be no commandementes expressly set out concerning the duties of euery seuerall man, yet forasmuch as the law commaundeth to *geue to euery man his owne, it doth in a
summe comprise all the partes and duties of euery man priuately in his degree and trade of life.
And in these tables, the Lord hath briefely and
summarily comprehended all those thynges
which in the scriptures are elce where most
largely set out concerning the seuerall commaundementes and duties of euery seuerall man.

Ma. Seing then the law doth shew a perfect maner
of worshipping God aright, ought we not to liue
wholly according to the rule thereof?

Sch. Yea, and so much that God * promiseth life to them that liue according to the rule of
the law, and on the other side * threatneth death
to them that breake hys law, as is aforesayd. And
for thys cause in my diuision I haue named obe-

                F.iiij.   dience

dience as one of the principall partes of religion.

Ma. Doest thou then thinke them to be iustified
that do in all thinges obey the law of God?

Sch. Yea surely, if any were able to performe it,
they should be iustified by the law, but we * are
all of such weakenesse that no man in all poyntes
fulfilleth hys dutie. For, though we put case that
there be one founde that performeth the law
in some poynt, yet shall he not thereby be iustified
before God, for he pronounceth them all to be
* accursed and abhominable that do not fulfill all
thinges that are conteined in the law.

Ma. Doest thou then determine, that no mortall
man is iustified before God by the law?

Sch. No man. For the * scriptures do also pronounce the same.

Ma. Why then did God make such a law as requireth a perfect on aboue our habilitie?

Sch. In making the law, God respected not so
much what we were hable to performe, which
by our owne fault * are very weake, as what
was meete for his owne righteousnesse. And forasmuch as none but the hyest * righteousnesse
could please God, it behoued that the rule of life
which he set out should be throughly perfect.
Moreouer the law requireth nothing of vs but
that we are bound to performe. But sithe we
are farre from due * obeying the law, men can
haue no sufficient or lawfull excuse to defend
them selues before God, & so the law accuseth all
men for gilty, yea * and condemneth them before the iudgement seate of God: and that is the
cause why Paul calleth the law the ministerie of
death and damnation.

                           Ma.

Ma. Doth then the law set all men in this most remedilesse estate?

Sch. The vnbeleuing and the vngodly the law doth both set and leaue in such case as I haue spoken, who as they are not hable to fulfill the least iote of the law, so haue they no affiance at all in God through Christ. But among the godly the law hath other vses.

Ma. What vses?

Sch. First the law in requiring so precise perfectnesse of life, doth shew to the godly as it were a marke for them to leuell at, & a goale to runne vnto, that dayly profiting they may with earnest endeuor trauaile toward the hyest vprightnesse. This purpose and desire the godly by the guyding of God do conceiue. But principally they take heede, so much as they are hable to do and atteine to, that it may not be sayd that there is any notorious fault in them. Secondly, whereas the law requireth thinges farre aboue mans power, and where they finde them selues to weake for so great a burden, the law doth rayse them vp to craue strength at ye Lordes hand. Moreouer, when the law doth continually accuse them, it striketh their hart with a holesome sorrow, and driueth them to the repentance that I spake of, and to begge and obteyne pardon of God through Christ, and therwithall restrayneth them that they trust not vpon theyr owne innocencie, nor presume to be proude in the sight of God, and is alway to them as a bridle, to withholde them in the feare of God. Finally when beholding by the law, as it were in a glasse, the spottes and vncleannesse of theyr

G.j. soules,

soules, they learne thereby that they are not able to atteyne perfect righteousnesse ˙ by theyr workes, by this meane they are trayned to humilitie, and so the law prepareth them and sendeth them to seeke righteousnesse in Christ.

Ma. Then, as farre as I perceiue, thou sayest that ˙the law is as it were a certayne schoolemaster to Christ, to leade vs the right way to Christ, by knowing of our selues, and by repentance and fayth.

Sch. Yea forsothe.

The second part. Of the Gospell and Faith.

Ma. Sithe now my dere childe, thou hast, so much as it may be in a short abridgement, largely answered this matter of the Law and Obedience, good order requireth that we speake next of the Gospell, which conteineth the promises of God, and promiseth the mercie of God through Christ to them that haue broken Gods law, and to the which Gospell faith hath specially respect. For this was the second point in our diuision, and this also the very orderly course of those matters that we haue treated of, hath as it were brought vs by the hand vnto. What is now the summe of the Gospell and of our Faith?

Sch. Euen the same wherin the chiefe articles of the Christian faith, haue bene in olde tyme briefly knitte vp & conteined, and which is commonly called the Crede or Symbole of the Apostles.

Ma. Why is the sume of our faith called a Symbole?

Sch. A Symbole by interpretation is a badge, marke, watchword, or token, whereby the soldiers of one side are knowen from the enemics. For which cause the short summe of our faith, by which the Christians are seuerally knowen from them

them that be not Christians, is rightly called a Symbole.

Ma. But why is it called the Symbole of the Apostles?

Sch. Bicause it was first receiued from the Apostles owne mouth, or most faithfully gathered out of their writings, and allowed from the very beginning of the Chirch, and so hath continually remained among all the godly firme, stedfast, and vnremoued, as a sure and stayed rule of Christian faith.

Ma. Go to. I would haue thee now rehearse to me the Symbole it selfe.

Sch. J will. *I beleue in God the Father almightie, maker of heauen & earth. And in Iesus Christ his onely Sonne our Lord. Which was conceaued by the holy Ghost, borne of the Virgin Mary. Suffred vnder Ponce Pylate, was crucified, dead, and buryed. He descended into Hell. The third day he rose againe from the dead. He ascended into heauen, and sitteth at the right hand of God the father almightie. From thence shall he come to iudge the quicke & the dead. I beleue in the holy Ghost. The holy Catholike Chirch. The Communion of Saintes. The forgeueneße of sinnes. The Resurrection of the body. And the life euerlasting. Amen.*

Ma. These thinges, my childe, thou hast briefly and in short summe set forth. Wherefore it is good that thou declare more plainely and at large what thou thinkest of euery particular. And first into how many partes doest thou diuide this whole confession of fayth?

Sch. Jnto fower principall partes, in the first whereof is entreated of God the Father, and the creation of all thinges: in the second, of his sonne Iesus Christ, which part also conteineth

G.ij.   the

the whole summe of the redemption of man : in the third, of the holy Ghost: in the fourth, of ẙ Chirch and of the benefites of God toward the Chirch.

Ma. Goe forward then to declare me those fower partes in order. And first, in the very beginning of the Creede, what meanest thou by this word *Beleue?*

Sch. I meane thereby that I haue a true and a liuely faith , that is to say , * a Christian mans faith in God the Father , the Sonne, ꝗ the Holy Ghost, and that I do by this forme of confession * testifie and approue the same faith.

Ma. Is there any faith that is not a true and a liuely Faith.

Sch. There is in deede a certaine generall faith, as I may so call it, and there is * a dead faith.

Ma. Sithe then it is a mater of no small weight that thou comprehendest vnder the name of Beleuing, and of a Christian fayth , that is to say , a true and liuely fayth, goe to and tell me what faith that same is, and how it differeth from the generall fayth, and also from the dead fayth.

Sch. The generall fayth is that which * crediteth the worde of God, that is, which beleueth all those thinges to be true that are conteined in the Scriptures concerning God , his incomprehensiblenesse, power, righteousnesse, wisedome, mercy toward the faithfull ꝗ godly, and most earnest seueritie toward the vnbeleuing ꝗ vngodly , and likewise all other things taught in the scriptures.

Ma. Doth not the true fayth that thou speakest of, beleue also all these same thinges?

Sch. Yea forsooth . But the true fayth goeth further, as I shall shewe byandby . * For thus farre not onely vngodly men, but also the very

Deuils

* Mat.18.b.19.
Rom.1.b.17.
Iob.1.b.12.13.
Gal.3.b.16.

* Mat.10.c.38.
Rom.10.b.9.
Heb.4.b.14.

* Rom.1.b.32.
Tit.2.b.16.
Iacob.6.b.26.

* Mat.7.b.20.
Luc.12.f.42.
2.Cor.13.d.5.

* Rom.1.b.32.
Tit.1.b.16.
Iac.2.b.19.

deuils do beleue, and therefoꝛe neither are they
* in deede faithfull, noꝛ are ſo called. But the
true fayth, as it nothyng douteth that all things
taught in the woꝛde of God are moſt certainely
true, * ſo doth it alſo embꝛace the pꝛomiſes made
concerning the mercy of God the Father, and the
foꝛgeuenesſe of ſinnes to the faythfull thꝛough
Jeſus Chꝛiſt, which pꝛomiſes are pꝛoperly called
* the Goſpell . Which fayth who ſoeuer haue,
they do not onely feare * God as the moſt mighty Loꝛde of all , and the moſt righteous iudge
(which we already ſayd that the moſt part of the
vngodly and the * deuils them ſelues do) but alſo they loue him as their moſt bountifull and
mercifull * father . Whom as they trauaile in all
thynges to pleaſe (as becommeth) obedient childꝛen) with godly endeuoꝛs and woꝛkes, which
are called the fruites of fayth, ſo haue they à good
and ſure hope, of * obteyning pardon thꝛough
Chꝛiſt, when, as men, they ſwarue from his will.
Foꝛ they know that, Chꝛiſt (whom they truſt
vpon) * appeaſing the wꝛath of hys father, their
ſinnes ſhall neuer be imputed any moꝛe vnto
them than if the ſame had neuer ben committed.
And though them ſelues haue not ſatiſfied the
lawe, and their dutie toward God and men , yet
beleue they that Chꝛiſt with hys moſt full obſeruing of the law, hath abundantly ſatiſfied God
foꝛ them , and are perſwaded that by thys hys
* righteouſnesſe and obſeruing of the law of God,
them ſelues are accompted in the number and
ſtate of the righteous, ꝗ that they are beloued of
God, euen as if them ſelues had fulfilled the law.
And this is the * iuſtification, which the holy

          G.iij.   Scriptures

Scriptures do declare that we obteine by fayth.

Ma. Can not these thinges also be in the deuils, or in wicked men?

Sch. Nothyng lesse. For * though they feare, or rather with horror do dread God as most mighty and righteous, for that they know he will take vengeaunce of their vngodlinesse, yet can they neither haue any trust in hys goodnesse and mercy toward them, nor any recourse to hys grace, nor enter into any endeuour to obey hys will. Therefore their fayth, although they dout not of the truth of the worde of God, is called * a dead fayth, for that like a drye and dead stocke it neuer bringeth forth any fruites of godly life, that is, of loue to God, and charitie toward men.

Ma. Geue me then out of that which thou hast hetherto sayd, a definition of that same liuely true and Christian faith.

Faith defined.

Sch. * Faith is an assured knowledge of the fatherly good will of God toward vs through Christ and an affiance in the same goodnesse, as it is witnessed in the Gospell, which faith hath coupled with it an * endeuour of godly life, that is, to obey the will of God the father.

Ma. Thou hast sufficiently declared, what thou meanest by the termes of Faith and Beleuing. Now goe forward and tell me in as apt wordes as thou cannest what thou vnderstandest by the name of God, which foloweth next in the Creede.

Sch. I will do the best I can, good master, as my wit and habilitie will serue me. I vnderstand that there is * one nature, or * substance, or soule, or minde, or rather * diuine spirite, (for diuersly haue wisemen both Heathen and Christian termed

med God, where in deede by no wordes he can be properly termed) * eternall, without beginning and end, * vnmeasurable, * vncorporall, inuisible with the eyes of men, of * most excellent maiesty, which we call God, whom all peoples of the world * must reuerence, and worship with hyest honor, and in him as in the best and greatest * to settle their hope and assiance.

Ma. Seing there is but one God, tell me why in the confession of the Christian fayth thou rehearsest three, the Father, the Sonne, and the Holy Ghost.

Sch. Those be not the names of * sondry Gods, but of three distinct persons in one Godhed. For in * one substance of God, we must consider, the * *Father* which of him selfe begat the Sonne euen from eternitie, the beginning and first author of all thinges: the * *Sonne*, euen from eternitie begotten of the Father, which is the eternall wisedome of God the Father: the * *Holy Ghost* proceeding from them both, as the power of God spred abroade through all thinges, but yet so as it also continually abideth in it selfe:and * yet that God is not therefore diuided. For of these three persons none goeth before the other * in time, in greatnesse, nor in dignitie: but the Father, the Sonne, and the Holy Ghost, three distinct persons * in eternitie of like continuance, in power eeuen, in dignitie egall, & in godhead one. There is therefore * one eternall, immortall, almightie, glorious, the best, the greatest, God the Father, the Sonne, and the Holy Ghost. For so hath the bniuersall number of Christians, which is called the catholike chirch, * taught vs by the holy scriptures, concerning God the Father, the Sonne,

          G.iiij.   and

and the Holy Ghost: where otherwise the infinite
depth of thys mysterie is so great that it can not
with minde be conceiued, much lesse with wordes
be expressed, wherin therefore is required a simplicitie of Christian fayth redy to beleue, rather
* than sharpenes of witte to search, or the office of
the tong to expresse so secret & hidden a mistery.

Ma. Thou sayest true. Goe forward therfore. Why
doest thou call God Father?

Sch. Beside the same principall cause which I
haue alredy rehearsed, which is, for that he is the
* naturall father of his onely sonne, begotten of
him selfe from before all beginning, there be
two other causes why he both is in deede and
is called our Father. * The one is, for that
he first created vs, and gaue life vnto vs all.
* The other cause is of greater value, namely
for that he hath heauenly begotten vs agayne
through the holy Ghost, and * by fayth in his true
and naturall sonne Iesus Christ he hath adopted vs his children, and through the same Christ
hath geuen vs his kingdome and the inheritance
of euerlasting life.

Ma. In what sense doest thou geue hym the name
of *Almighty?*

Sch. For that, * as he hath created the world & all
thinges, so he hath the same in his power, gouerneth them by his prouidence, ordereth them after
his owne will, and commaundeth all as it plea-
seth him: so as there is nothing done but by hys
apointment or sufferance, and nothing is there
which he is not hable to do: for I do not imagine
God to haue a certayne idle power which he
putteth not in vse.

* Pro. 1. b. 16.

The first part
of the Crede.
God the father.
* Mat. 3. c. 17.
Ioh. 1. b. 14.
Rom. 15. b. 6.
2. Cor. 1. a. 3. & 11. g. 31.

* Gen. 1. b. 27.
Mal. 1. c. 6. & 2. b. 10.

* Ioh. 3. a. 3. 5.
1. Pet. 1. a. 3. b. 23.

* Ioh. 1. b. 12.
Rom. 8. c. 15. 17. b. 23.
& 9. 4.
Gal. 4. a. 5. 6.
Eph. 1. a. 5. 6.
Tit. 3. b. 7.

* Esa. 40. c. 21.
Mat. 19. g. 41. & 10. c. 29
Eph. 1. b. 19.

Ma.

Ma. Doeſt thou then make vngodly men alſo and wicked ſpirites ſubiectes to the power of God?

Sch. * Why not? for els were we in moſt miſerable caſe, for that we ſhould neuer be out of feare if they might haue any power ouer vs without the will of God. But God, as it were with the bridle of his power, ſo reſtreineth them þ they can not once ſtirre but at his becke & ſufferance. And we for our partes are vpholden with this comfort, that we are ſo in the power of our almighty Father, that not ſo much as * one heare of ours can periſh but by hys will that beareth vs ſo good will.

Ma. Goe forward.

Sch. * Foraſmuch as the minde of man is not able of it ſelfe to conceiue the goodneſſe & incomprehenſiblenes of moſt good & moſt great God, we adde further that he is the Creator of heauen & earth & of al things conteined in them. By which wordes we ſignifie that God is, as it were in a glaſſe, to be beholden, and (ſo farre as behoueth vs) to be knowen in his workes and in the orderly * courſe of the world. For when we ſee that ſame vnmeaſurable greatneſſe of the world and all the partes thereof to be ſo framed, as they could not poſſibly in beauty be fayrer, nor for profit be better, we forthwith thereby vnderſtand the infinite power, wiſdome, and goodneſſe of the workeman and builder thereof. For who is ſo brutiſh, that in looking vp to heauen doth not perceiue that there is a God? Yea for this cauſe ſpecially it ſemeth that God hath faſhioned men out of the earth, tall, and vpright, that they ſhould be beholders of thinges aboue & heauen-

ly matters, and in beholding heauen might conceiue the knowledge of him.

Ma. How doest thou say that God created al things?

Sch. *That God the most good and mighty Father, at the beginning and of nothing * by the
power of his word, that is, of Iesus Christ hys
sonne, framed and made this whole visible world
and all thinges whatsoeuer they be that are conteined therin, and * also the vncorporall spirites,
whom we call Angels.

Ma. But doest thou thinke it godly to affirme, that
God created all spirites, euen those wicked spirites,
whom we call diuelles?

Sch. God did not * create them such, but they by
theyr owne euillnesse, fell from theyr first creation, without hope of recouery, and so are they
become euill, not by creation and nature, but by
corruption of nature.

Ma. Did God thinke it enough to haue once created all thinges, and then to cast away all further care
of thinges from thence forth?

Sch. I haue alredy briefly touched thys point.
Whereas it is much more excellent to mainteine
and preserue thynges created, than to haue once
created them: we must certainly beleue, * that
when he had so framed the world & al creatures,
he from thence forth hath preserued & yet preserueth them. For all things would runne to ruine,
and fall to nothyng, vnlesse by hys vertue, & as it
were by hys hand, they were vpholden. We also
assuredly beleue *that the whole order of nature,
and changes of thinges which are falsely repu-
ted the alterations of fortune, do hang all vpon
God: * that God guideth the course of the heauen

den, vpholdeth the earth, tempereth the seas, and
ruleth this whole world, and that all thinges o-
bey his diuine power, and by his diuine power
all thinges are gouerned : that he is the * author
of fayre weather and of tempest, of raine and of
drowth, of frutefulnesse, of barennesse, of health
and of sicknesse : that of all thinges that belong
to the sustentation and preseruing of our life, and
which are desired either for necessary vse or honest pleasure, finally of all thinges that nature
nedeth, he hath euer geuen and yet most largely
geueth abundance and plenty with most liberall
hand : to this end verily, that we should so vse
them as becommeth mindefull & kinde children.

Ma. To what end doest thou thinke that almighty
God hath created all these thinges.

Sch. The world it selfe * was made for Man,
and all thinges that are therein were prouided
for the vse and profit of men. And as God made
all other thinges for man, * so made he man himselfe for his owne glory.

Ma. What hast thou then to say of the first beginning and creation of Man?

Sch. That which Moses wrote, that is : That
God * fashioned the first Man of clay, and brea-
thed into him soule and life : and afterward out
of the side of Man being cast in a slepe, to take
out woman and brought her into the world,
to ioyne her to man for a companion of his
life. And therefore was * Man called Adam,
because he tooke hys beginning of the earth:
and * Woman was called Eua, because she
was ordeined to be the mother of all lyuing
persones.

Ma. Where at thys day there is to be seen in both
sortes both men and women, so great corruption,
wickednesse, & peruersenesse, dyd God create them
such from the beginning?

Sch. Nothyng lesse. For God being most perfectly good, can make nothyng * but good. God therfore at the first, made man according to his owne
* image and likenesse.

Ma. What is that Image, according to the which
thou sayest that Man was fashioned?

Sch. It is most absolute righteousnesse, and most
perfect holinesse, which most properly belongeth
to the very nature of God: and which hath bene
most euidently shewed * in Christ our new A-
dam, and wherof, in vs there now scant appeare
any sparcles.

Ma. Yea? do there scant appeare any?

Sch. Yea truely. For they do not now so shine, as
at the beginning before the fall of Man, because
Man *with darknesse of sinnes, & mist of errors,
hath extinguished the brightnesse of that image.

Ma. But tell me how thys came to passe.

Sch. I will tell you. When the Lorde God had
made thys world, * he prepared a most finely
trimmed garden, and most full of delite & plea-
santnesse, euery where abounding with all delitefull thinges that might be wished. Herein
the Lord God, for a certaine singular good will,
placed man, & allowed him the vse of all thinges:
onely * he forbad him the fruite of the tree of
knowledge of good and euill, threatening hym
with death, if he once tasted of it. For reason it
was that man * hauing receaued so many beni-
fites should in so farre obeying shew himself willingly

* Gen. 1.b.31.

* Gen. 1.b.26.
Colo. 3.b.10.

* Rom.1.f.29.
2.Cor.15.f.49.
3.Cor.3.b.18.&4.&6.
Colo.2.b.15.&3.b.10.

* Rom.1.c.21.
2.Cor.1.c.18.23.&2.b.
14.&3.b.19.
Ephe.4.b.17.

* Gen.2.b.8.

* Gen.2.d.17.

* Gen.3.b.11.
Psal.1.b.4.5.6.&c.

lingly obedient to the commandement of God,
and that being contented with his owne estate,
he should not, being himselfe a creature, auance
himself hyer against the wil of his creator.

Ma. What then folowed?

Sch. The woman * deceiued by the deuill, perswaded the man to taste the forbidden fruite,
which thing made them both forthwith subiect
to death. And that heauenly image according to
which he was first created, being defaced, in
place of wisdome, strength, holinesse, truth and
righteousnesse, the iewelles wherewith God had
adorned him, there succeeded the most horrible
plages, * blindnesse, weakenesse, vaine lying, and
vnrighteousnesse, in which euils and miseries
he also wrapped and ouerwhelmed his issue and
all his posteritie.

Ma. But may it not seeme that God did too rigo-
rously punish the tasting of one apple?

Sch. Let no man extenuate the most hainous
offence of man as a small trespasse, * and wey the
deede by the apple and the onely excesse of glutto-
nie. For he with his wife, enticed & alured with
the gilefull * allurementes of Satan, by infidelitie reuolted from the truth of God to a lie: he
gaue credite to the false suggestions of the Serpent, wherin he accused God of vntruth, of enuie,
& of malicious withdrawing of some goodnesse:
hauing receiued so many benefites, * he became
most vnthankfull toward the geuer of them: he
the issue of the earth, not contented that he was
made according to ỹ image of God, with * intolerable ambition and pride sought to make himself
egall with the maiestie of God. Finally * he with-

        H.iij.   drew

drew himselfe from allegeance to his creator, yea
and malepertly shoke of his yoke. Vaine therfore
it is to extenuate the sinne of Adam.

Ma. But how can it seme but vnrighteous, that for
the parentes fault, all the posteritie should be depri-
ued of soueraigne felicitie, and burdened with extreme euilles and miseries?

Sch. Adam was the first parent of mankinde.
Therefore God endued him with those orna-
mentes, to haue them or lose them for him & his,
that is, for all mankinde. So soone as he therfore
was spoyled of them, his whole nature was left
naked, in penury & destitute of all good thinges.

So soone as he was defiled with that spot
of sinne, *out of the roote & stock corrupted, there
sprong forth corrupted branches, that conueyed
also their corruption into the other twigges
springing out of them. Thence it came that so
short, *small, and vncertaine race of life is limited
vnto vs. Thence came the infirmitie of our flesh,
* the feblenesse of our bodies, the weakenesse and
frailenesse of mankinde. Thence came the horrible *blindnesse of our mindes, and peruersnesse of
our hartes. Thence came that crookednesse, and
corruptnesse of all our affections and desires.
Thence came that * seedeplot, and as it were a
sincke of all sinnes, with the faultes wherof
mankinde is infected and tormented. Of which
euill, learned Christians that haue sought y proper & true name, haue called it Originall sinne.

Ma. Doth mankind suffer the punishmentes of this
sinne in this life onely?

Sch. No. But mans nature hath bene so corrupted and destroyed with this natiue mischief, that
                if

* Rom. 5. b. 12. 14. & 17.
18. &c.
1. Cor. 15. c. 22. q. g. 48.

* Psal. 100. a. 3. 6. 7. b.
9. 10. & 103. b. 8. 9. &
109. 23. q8.

* Job. 14. a. 1. q2.

* Rom. 1. c. 21.
1. Cor. 3. f. 17. 11.
Ephe. 4. d. 18. 19.

* Rom. 5. b. 12. q8.

if the goodnesse and * mercie of almighty God
had not, with applying a remedie, holpen & releued vs in affliction, like as we fell in our wealth
into all calamities, & in our bodies into all * miseries of diseases and of death, so should we of necessitie fall hedlong * into darknesse and euerlasting night, and into fire vnquenchable, there
with all kinde of punishment to be perpetually
tormented. And no maruell it is, that * other creatures also incurred that paine which man deserued, for whose vse they were created. And the
whole order of nature being troubled both * in
heauen & in earth), harmefull tempestes, barrennesse, diseases, and infinite other euills, brake into the world, * into which miseries and woes,
beside the sayd natiue mischiefe, we by our owne
many & great sinnes are most deseruedly fallen.

Ma. O deadly and horrible plage and calamitie by
sinne! But what remedie is that which thou sayest
that God hath prouided for vs, wherein our forefa-
thers, and from thense forth all their posteritie, haue
set and setled their hope?

Sch. Forsooth, they were comfortably raised to
that hope of saluation which they haue conceiued of faith in Iesus Christ the deliuerer and sauiour promised them of God. For that is it which
now followeth next in the Creede: *I beleue in Iesus Christ. &c.*

Ma. Did God geue also to our first parentes byandby hope of deliuerance by Iesus Christ?

Sch. Yea. For as he thrust * Adam and Eue out of
the garden, after that he had first sharply chasti-
sed them with wordes, so he cursed the Serpent,
and thretened him * that the time should one day
         H.iiij.   come

come, when the seede of the woman should broose his head.

Ma. What seede is that, whereof God speaketh?

Sch. That same seede * is (as sainct Paul plainly teacheth vs) Jesus Christ the sonne of God very God, and the sonne of the virgin very man, in whom we professe in the second part of the Creede, that we settle our hope and confidence: which was * conceiued of the Holy Ghost, and borne of the nature of the holy, chast, and vndefiled virgin Mary, and of the same mother he was so borne, and nourished, as other infants be, * sauing that he was altogether pure and free from all contagion of sinne.

Ma. Did God thinke it sufficient once in the olde Testament to haue made promise of this seede?

Sch. No. But this most ioyfull promise to mankinde, * which was first made to our parentes, the Lord God did oft confirme to their posteritie, to the end that men should haue the greater expectation of the performance of it. For after he had * entred into couenant by circumcision with Abraham and his seede, he confirmed hys promise first to Abraham himselfe, & then to Isaac hys sonne, and after to Jacob his sonnes sonne. Last of all with most euident oracles vttered *by Moses and hys other Prophetes, he continued and maintained the assurednesse of his promise.

Ma. What meane these wordes: *To broose the Serpentes head?*

Sch. In * the head of the Serpent hys poyson is conteyned, and the substance of hys life and strength consisteth. Therefore the Serpentes head signifieth the whole strength, power, and
kingdome,

* Gal. 3. c. 16. 19.

* Mat. 1. b. 20. 23.
Luc. 1. b. 31. 35.

* Joh. 1. d. 29.
Heb. 4. d. 15. & 9. b. 14.

* Gen. 3. a. 14. 15.

* Gen. 17. b. 10. & 22. b.
18. & 26. a. 4. & 28. c. 14.

* Deu. 19. c. 15. & 34.
a. 4.
Psal. 89. a. 4. c. 35.
Esa. 53. & 54. a. 3. & 63.
b. 9.

* Psal. 74. c. 13. & 140.
a. 1. &
Eccle. 10. b. 10.
Amos 9. a. 3.

kyngdome, oz rather the tyzannie of the deuill the
old serpent : *all which, Jesus Chzist , that same
sede of the woman , in whom God hath perfoz=
med the full sume of his pzomise, hath subdued by
the bertue of his death . And so in bzeakyng the
serpentes hed , he hath rescued & made free from
tyzannie, all them that trust in him . Foz this is
it which we here pzofesse in the Crede, that we
BELEVE IN IESVS CHRIST THE SONNE
OF GOD, that is, that Jesus Chzist is the deliue=
rer & sauiour of vs which were holden bond and
fast tyed with impietie & wickednesse, and wzap=
ped in the snares of eternall death , and holden
thzall in soule bondage of the serpent the deuill.
Ma. It semeth me that thou hast expounded the
name of IESVS with a verie plaine declaration.
Sch. It is true . Foz IESVS in Hebzew sig=
nifieth none other, than, in Greke SOTER, in
Latin SERVATOR, & in English a SAVIOVR.
Foz they haue no fitter name to expzesse the fozce
& signification therof. And by this that we haue
sayd, it can not now be vnknowen, why he had
this name . Foz he alone hath deliuered & saued
them that be his from eternall damnation, wher=
unto otherwise they were apointed. Some other
in dede haue taken vpon them this name, bicause
it was thought that they had saued some mens
bodies, *but Jesus Chzist alone is able to saue
both soules and bodies of them that trust in him.
Ma. Who gaue him this name?
Sch. The Angel by the commaundement of
God him selfe. And * also it was of necessitie, that
he should in deede answere and perfozme the

    I.j.   name

name that God had geuen him.

Ma. Now tell me what meaneth the name of Chrift.

Sch. It is as much to say, as * Anointed, wherby is meant that he is the soueraigne kyng, Priest, and Prophet.

Ma. How shall that appeare?

Sch. By the holy Scripture, * which both doth applie anointing to these three offices, and doth also oft attribute the same offices to Chrift.

Ma. Was then Chrift anointed with oile, such as they vsed at creation of kynges, priestes, and prophetes in old tyme?

Sch. No. But with much more excellent oile, namely * with the most plentifull grace of the holy ghost wherewith he was filled, and * most abundantly endued with hys diuine richesse. Of which heauenly anoynting, that outward anoynting was but a shadow.

Ma. Obteined he these thinges for him selfe alone, or doth he also geue vs any commodities therby?

Sch. Yea, Chrift receiued these thynges of his father, to the intent that he should communicate the same vnto vs, in such measure and maner as he knew to be most mete for euery of vs. For * out of hys fullnesse, as out of the onely, holy, and euer encreasing noble fountaine, we all do draw all the heauenly good thynges that we haue.

Ma. Doeft thou not then say that Chriftes kyngdome is a worldly kingdome?

Sch. No: but * a spirituall and eternall kyngdome, that is gouerned and ordered by the word
and

and spirit of God, which bring with them righteousnesse and life.

Ma. What fruite take we of this kingdome?

Sch. It furnisheth vs with * strength and spirituall armour to vanquish the flesh , the world,
sinne, and the diuell , the outragious and deadly
enimies of our soule : it geueth vs blessed freedome of consciences: finally it endoweth vs with
heauenly richesse , and comforteth and strength-
neth vs to liue godlily and holily.

Ma. What maner of Priest is Christ?

Sch. The * greatest and an euerlasting priest,
which onely is hable to appeare before God,
onely hable to make the sacrifice that God will
allowe and accept , and onely hable to appease
the wrath of God.

Ma. To what commoditie of ours doth he this?

Sch. For * vs he craueth and prayeth peace and
pardon of God, for vs he appeaseth the wrath of
God, and vs he reconcileth to his father . For
Christ alone is our Mediator, by whom we are
made at one with God. Yea he maketh vs as it
were * fellow priestes with hym in his priest-
hoode, geuing vs also an entrie to his father that
we may with assurednesse come into hys presence, and be bold by him to offer vs and all ours
to God the father in sacrifice.

Ma. What maner of Prophet is Christ?

Sch. Whereas men did * despise and reiect the
prophetes the seruantes of almighty God, sent
before by hym selfe to teach mortall men his will,
and had with their owne dreames and inuentions darkened and drowned hys holy word , he

J.ij.   himselfe

himselfe the sonne of God, the lord of all prophets came downe into this world, that fully declaring the will of his father, he might make an end of all prophecies and foretellinges. He therefore came * hys fathers embassador and messinger to men, that by hys declaration they might be brought into the right knowledge of God and into all truth. So in the name of CHRIST are conteined those three offices which the sonne of God receiued of his father and fulfilled, to make vs parteners with him of all the fruite therof.

Ma. It semeth then that in a summe thou sayest thus, that the sonne of God is not only called and is in dede IESVS CHRIST, that is, the Sauiour, King, Priest, and Prophet, but also that he is so for vs and to our benefit and saluation.

Sch. It is true.

Ma. But sith this honor is geuen to * all the godly, to be called the children of God, how doest thou call Christ the onely sonne of God?

Sch. God is * the naturall father of Christ alone, and Christ alone is naturally the sonne of God, being begotten of the substance of the father, and being of one substance with the father. But vs hath God freely through Christ made and adopted his children. Therefore we rightly acknowledge Christ the only sonne of God, sith this honor is by his owne and most iust right due vnto him: yet the * name of children by right of adoption is also freely imparted to vs through Christ.

Ma. Now how doest thou vnderstand that he is our Lord?

Sch.

Sch. For that the Father hath geuen hym * dominion ouer men, angels, and all things, and for that he gouerneth the kingdome of God both in heauen and in earth, with hys owne will and power. And hereby are all the godly put in minde, that they are not * at their owne libertie, but that both in their bodies and ſoules, and in their life and death), they are wholly ſubiect to their Lorde, to whom they ought to be obedient and ſeruiceable, in all thinges, as moſt faythfull ſeruantes.

Ma. What foloweth next?

Sch. Next is declared how he tooke vpon him mans nature, and hath perfomed all thinges needefull to our ſaluation.

Ma. Was it then neceſſarie that the ſonne of God ſhould be made man?

Sch. Yea. For * neceſſary it was that what man had offended agaynſt God, man ſhould abye and ſatiſfie it, which moſt heauy burden none but * the man Jeſus Chriſt was able to take vp and beare. And other * mediator could there not be to ſet men at one with God, and to make peace betwene them but Jeſus Chriſt both God and man. Therefore being made man he did as it were put vpon him our perſon, that he might therein take vpon him, beare, perfome and fulfill the partes of our ſaluation.

Ma. But why was he conceiued of the holy ghoſt, and borne of the virgin Mary, rather than begotten after the vſuall and naturall maner?

Sch. It behoueth that he that ſhould and could ſatiſfie for ſinnes, and entierly reſtore wicked and

           J.iij.   Damned

damned perſons, ſhould not hymſelfe * be defiled
oʒ blemiſhed with any ſtayne oʒ ſpot of ſinne,
but be endewed with ſingular and perfect vp-
rightneſſe and innocencie. Therefoʒe when the

ſeede of man was wholy * coʒrupt and defyled, it
behoued that in conception of the ſonne of God
there ſhould be the maruellous and ſecret woʒ-
king of the holy Ghoſt whereby he might be fa-

ſhioned * in the wombe of the moſt chaſt and
pure virgin, and of her ſubſtance, that he ſhould
not be defiled with the common ſtayne and in-

fection of mankinde. Chriſt therfoʒe that * moſt
pure lambe, was begotten and boʒne by the holy Ghoſt and the conception of the virgin without ſinne, that he might cleanſe, waſh, and put
away our ſpottes, who as we were firſt conceiued and boʒne in ſinne and vncleanneſſe, ſo do
ſtill from thenſe foʒth continue in vncleane life.

Ma. But why is there in this Chriſtian confeſſion,
mention made by name of the virgin Marie?

Sch. That he may be knowne to be that * true
ſeede of Abraham and Dauid, of whom it was
from God foʒetolde and foʒeſhewed by the pʒo-
phecies of the pʒophetes.

Ma. By this that hath bene ſayd, I perceaue that
Ieſus Chriſt the ſonne of God did put on mans nature for ſaluation of men. Now goe forward. What
was done next?

Sch. That ſame moſt ioyfull and altogether
heauenly doctrine of reſtoʒing ſaluation by
Chriſt, which doctrine is in Greeke called *Euan-*

gelion, the Goſpell oʒ glad tydinges, * which in
olde tyme was diſcloſed by the holy pʒophetes
the

the ſeruauntes of God, * he him ſelfe at length the Lord of prophetes Jeſus Chriſt the ſonne of God and alſo of the virgin, euen the ſame promiſed ſeede, hath moſt clerely taught all men, and * commaunded his Apoſtles, whom hee choſe for that purpoſe, to teach the ſame throughout the whole world.

Ma. Did he thinke it enough to haue ſimply and plainely taught this doctrine in wordes?

Sch. No. But, to the end that men ſhould with more willyng myndes embrace it, he confirmed and approued the ſame * with healing of diſeaſes, * chacing away deuilles, and with infinite other good dedes, miracles, and ſignes, wherof * both his owne life, and the life of his Apoſtles moſt innocently and holily ledde, was moſt plentifull.

Ma. But why doth the Crede omit the ſtorie of his life, and paſſeth ſtreight from his birth to his death?

Sch. Bicauſe in the Crede are rehearſed onely the * chiefe pointes of our redemption, and ſuch thinges as ſo properly belong to it, that they conteine as it were the ſubſtance therof.

Ma. Now tell me the order & maner of his death.

Sch. He was * wickedly betrayed and forſaken of his owne diſciples, falſly and maliciouſly accuſed of the Jewes, condemned by Pontius Pilate the iudge, cruelly beaten with ſore ſtripes, vilely handled and ſcorned, haled vp to the croſſe and faſtened vpon it, and ſo tormented with all extreme paines he ſuffered ſhamefull and moſt painefull death.

J.iiij.　　Ma.

Ma. Is this the thanke and recompence they gaue him for that heauenly doctrine, and for these most great and infinite benefites?

Sch. These thinges verily they did to him for their partes cruelly, maliciously, and wickedly. But he, * of his owne accord and willingly suffered and performed all these thinges, to the intent with this most swete sacrifice to appease his father toward mankinde, and * to pay and suffer the paines due to vs, and by this meane to deliuer vs from the same. Neither is it vnused among men, one to promise, and to be suertie, yea sometyme to suffer for an other. * But with Christ as our suertie, so sufferyng for vs, God dealt as it were with extremitie of law: but to vs whose sinnes, deseruynges, punishmentes, and due paines, he layed vpon Christ, he vsed singular lenitie, gentlenesse, clementie and mercie. Christ therfore suffred, and in suffering ouercame death, the paine appointed by the euerliuing God for mens offense. Yea and by his death he ouercame, subdued, ouerthrew, and vanquished hym that had the dominion of death, that is, * the deuill, from whose tyrannie and thraldome he rescued vs & set vs at libertie.

Ma. But sith we are neuerthelesse punished with death which daily hangeth ouer vs, and do still suffer the penaltie of our sinne, what frute receiue we of this victorie?

Sch. Surely most large frute. For by Christes death it is come to passe that to * the faithfull, death is now not à destruction, but as it were a remouing & chaunging of lyfe, & a very short and
sure

* Mat. 10. b. 18.
Marc. 10. f. 41.
Ioh. 10. b. 11. c. 15. 17. 18
Rom. 4. b. 21.
Colos. 1. c. 20.

* Esa. 53. tote.
2. Cor. 1. 21.
Gal. 1. a. 4.
Ephe. 1. b. 7.
Colos. 2. d. 14.

* Gen. 42. B. 19. a. 24. f.
57. g 43. b. 9. c. 23. g 44.
c. 16. b. 31. 33.

* Act. 10. f. 38.
Colos. 1. b. 13.
Heb. 2. B. 14.

* Luc. 23. f. 41.
Ioh. 11. c. 25. 26.

sure passage into heauen, whether we ought to folow our guide without feare, which as he was not destroyed by death, so will he also not suffer vs to perish . Wherfore the godly ought now no moze to shrinke oz quake * foz feare of death, which is to them the refuge from all the labozs, cares, and euilles of this lyfe, and their leader to heauen.

Ma. Commeth there any other profite to vs by the death of Christ?

Sch. In them that through fayth are of one bodie with Christ, croked * affections and corrupt desires, which we call the lustes of the fleshe, are as it were crucified with hym, and dye, so as they haue no moze dominion in our soules.

Ma. Why is the Romane gouernor, vnder whom he suffred, expressly named?

Sch. First the certaine expressing of the persons and tunes bringeth credite to the matter. Secondly the very thing it self declareth that Christ tooke our nature vpon hym at hys due time, the very time limited and appointed by God, that is, when the * scepter was transferred from the issue of Juda, to the Romanes, and * to foreine kinges that held the kingdome of sufferance vnder the Romane Empire. Moreouer it had bene long before foreshewed by God, that Christ shold be * deliuered to the Gentiles to execution, and shoulde suffer death by the iudges sentence.

Ma. Why so?

Sch. He beyng gyltlesse was condemned by the iudges sentence, that he myght * befoze the heauenly iugement seate acquite and entierly re-

store vs that were gylty, whose cause was conuicted and condemned by the iugement of God.
For if he had been murdered by theues, or slayne
with sword by priuate men in an vprore or sedi-
tion, such death could haue had no forme of sa-
tiffaction and recompense.

* Mat. 27. c. 19. 23.
Mart. 15. b. 10.
Luc. 23. b. 14.
Joh. 18. g. 38.

Ma. But Pilate * did beare witnesse of hys innocencie.

Sch. Pilate dyd well to beare such witnesse of
hym, * sith he euidently knew hym innocent.

* Esa. 53. a. 9.
Joh. 1. c. 29. 36.
1. Pet. 3. b. 18.

For if he had ben gylty, he had not ben fitt nor
mete to beare and pay the paines of the sinnes of
other, and to appease God toward sinners. But
the same Pilate accombred with the continuall
and agreable cryeng out of the Jewes, * and

* Mat. 27. c. 22.
Luc. 23. b. 18. 21. 23. 24.

weryed and ouercome with their importunate
outcries, did afterward accordyng to the peoples mynde and request condemne innocent
Christ. Wherby it is plaine that he was not punished for hys owne sinnes, * which were none

* Esa. 53. d. 4. 5.
1. Pet. 2. b. 24. c. 3. b. 18

at all in hym, nor suffered paines due to him self,
but did beare and pay the paines due to mens
wickednesse, not due to him selfe, which of hys
owne will he toke vpon hym, sufferyng for them
by hys willyng death, and with his owne giltlesse bloud washyng away the spottes of our
offenses.

Ma. But for what cause did the people so bitterly
and throughly hate a man of so great and singular
vprightnesse and innocencie?

* Mat. 27. b. 18.
Mart. 15. a. 10.

Sch. The * Priestes, Pharisees and Scribes,
burnyng with the fire of enuie, when they

* Mat. 17. b. 12.
Luc. 20. c. 19.
Joh. 5. a. 40. 47. g 11. d.
47.

could * not abyde the face and light of the truth,
*in-

* incenſed the hatred of the vnwiſe multitude agaynſt the reſcuer and defender of the truth.

Ma. Sithe he was condemned by the iudges ſentence, why doeſt thou ſay that he dyed of hys owne will?

Sch. If the Phariſees, Scribes, or other Jewes, or they all together, had had power of life and death vpon Chriſt, they had long before haſtened hys death, * for they oftentimes before had conſpired hys death and deſtruction. Yea and alſo where they had determined to differre the execution till an other tyme, becauſe the feaſt of * Sweete bread was now at hand, which feaſt the Jewes were accuſtomed yerely to kepe holy with moſt great religiouſneſſe and ſolemnitie, they could not bring that intent to paſſe, but that he ſuffred euen hard before the feaſt day, in a time moſt vnſeaſonable for them, but appointed by God for thys purpoſe. Whereby ſufficiently appeareth, that no gouernance of theſe thinges and times was in their hand and power, but that * of hys owne will, not compelled by any force, he ſuffered this death for our ſaluation.

Ma. Why did God ſpecially appoint that day for hys death?

Sch. That by the very time alſo it might be perceaued, that Chriſt is that * Paſcall Lambe, that is to ſay, the truely chaſte and pure lambe, that ſhould be ſlaine, and yelde him ſelfe the moſt acceptable ſacrifice to hys father for vs.

Ma. Sithe he had the power to chooſe hys owne death, why would he be crucified rather than ſuffer any other kinde of death?

K.ij.   Sch.

• Esa.53.b.16.
B)sa.1.b.19.&8.
Iohn.11.c.18.
Luc.23.b.37.
Ioh.4.b.14.

Sch. First for his fathers will, wherunto he *con-
formed himselfe, and which had bene long afore
in olde tyme vttered and declared by God by so
many prophecies, and oracles, signes and tokens. Moreouer his will was to suffer all extremitie for vs that had deserued all extremitie. For

• Deu.21.d.23.
Gal.3.b.13.

that kinde of death was all other * most accursed and abhominable, which death yet he chosely
chose to dye for vs, to the entent to take vpon
him selfe the greuous curse, wherein our sinnes
had bound vs, and thereby to deliuer vs from

• Esa.53. tota.
Psal.21.a.6.7.c.12.
13.&c.
Mat.26.g.67.&27.c.
31.26.28.b.34.38.d.
44.f.48.
Phil.2.a.7.8.

the same curse. For all * spitefull handelinges, all
reproches and tormentes for our saluation, he
compted light and as thinges of nought, and so
was contented to be despised, an abiect, and to
be accompted the basest of all men, that he might
restore vs, which were vtterly vndone, to the
hope of saluation that we had lost.

Ma. Hast thou any more to say of the death of
Christ?

• Esa.53.a.6.
Psal.22.a.1.
Mat.26.b.38.&27.f.
46.
Luc.22.b.44.

Sch. That Christ * suffered not only a common
death in sight of men, but also was touched with
the horror of eternall death: he fought & wrast-
led as it were hand to hand with the whole ar-
my of hell: before the iudgement seat of God he
put himselfe vnder the heauy iudgement and
greuous seueritie of Gods punishment: he was
driuen into most hard distresse: he for vs suffred
and went through horrible feares, and most bit-
ter greefes of minde, to satisfie Gods iust iudgement in all thinges and to appease his wrath.

• Esa.53.a.4.5.b.6.
1.Pet.2.b.18.

For * to sinners, whose person Christ did heare
beare, not only the sorrowes and paines of present

sent death are due, but also of death to come and
euerlasting. So when he did take vpon him and
beare both the giltinesse and iust iudgement of
mankinde which was vndone and alredy condemned, he was tormented with so great trouble and sorrow of minde, that * he cryed out, my
God, my God, why hast thou forsaken me?

Ma. Is not the sonne of God hereby dishonored,
and touched with some note of desperation?

Sch. He suffred all these thinges * without any
sinne, much lesse did any desperation possesse his
soule. For he neuer cessed in the meane time * to
trust in his father, and to haue good hope of hys
safetie. And being beset round about with feare
he was neuer dismayed or ouerwhelmed with
sorrow. And * wrestling with the whole power
of hell, he subdued and ouercame all the force
that stoode agaynst him, and all the furious and
violent assaultes. And all these he tooke vpon
him and vtterly destroyed them. And himselfe
remayned neuerthelesse most blessed, and inpar-
ted his blessednesse to vs that put our trust in
him. * For if we had not by this his blessed death
obteined saluation and life, we had all perished
for euer in euerlasting death.

Ma. But how could Christ being God, haue so great
sorrow of minde and fearefulnesse?

Sch. This came to passe according to the * state
of his humane nature, hys Godhed in the meane
time not putting forth the force of his power.

Ma. Now rehearse me briefely & in a summe these
most large benefites which the faythfull receiue of
the death of Christ and hys most greuous paine.

                K.iij.   Sch.

• Heb.7.b.11.& 9.d. 12.g 10.c.12.c.14.

• Rom.3.d.14. 1.Joh.1.b.7. Apoc.1.b.5.

• Psa.31.b.1.2. Rom.4.b.7.8. Heb.10.c.17.

• Colo.2.c.14.

• Joh.3.d.16.& 11.c.25. 26.

• Rom.6.a.4.7.b.11. &c. & 8.a.1.2.3.b.10. 11.&c. Colo.3.c.13.

• Esa.53.b.9. Mat.12.d.40.& 27.g. 50.60. 1.Cor.15.d.4.5.

Sch. Briefely, with the * one onely sacrifice of his death, he satisfied for our sinnes before God, and appeasing the wrath of God made vs at one with him: with his bloud as with * most pure washing, he hath washed and cleansed away all the filth and spottes of our soules : and defacing with euerlasting * forgetfulnesse the memorie of our sinnes that they shall no more come in the sight of God, he hath cancelled, made voyde, and done away the * handwriting wherby we were bound and conuicted, and also the decree by the sentence wherof we were condemned. All these thinges hath he done by his death, both for the lyuing, and for the dead * that trusted in him while they lyued. Finally by the strength of his death he so * bridleth and subdueth in them that cleaue wholly to him by fayth, the lustes which otherwise are vnbridled and vntamed, and so quencheth the burning heate of them, that they more easily obey and yelde to the spirit.

Ma. Why doest thou also adde that he was buried?

Sch. His * dead and spritelesse body was layed in graue, that his death should be more euident, & that all men might certainly know it. For if he had biandby reuiued, many would haue brought his death in debate and question, and so might it seme that it was likely to proue doutfull.

Ma. What meaneth that which foloweth of hys descending to hell?

Sch. That as Christ in his bodie descended into the bowels of the earth, so in hys soule seuered from the bodie he descended into hell : and that therewith also the vertue and efficacie of
his

hys death so pearced * through to the dead, and
to very hell it selfe, that both the soules of the
vnbeleuyng felt their most painefull and iust
* damnation for infidelitie, and Satan him selfe
the * prince of hell, felt that all the power of hys
tyrannie, and darkenesse, was weakened, vanquished, and fallen to ruine : on the other side,
* the dead which, while they liued, beleued in
Christ, vnderstode that the worke of their redemption was now finished, & vnderstode and
perceiued the effect and strength thereof with
most swete and assured comfort.

Ma. Now let vs go forward to the rest.

Sch. The thyrd day after, * he rose againe: and by
the space of fortye dayes oftentymes shewed him
selfe alyue to them that were hys, and was conuersant among hys disciples eatyng and drin-
king with them.

Ma. Was it not enough that by hys death we obteine deliuerance from sinne, and pardon?

Sch. That was not enough if ye consider either
hym or our selues. For if he had not risen agayne,
he could not be thought to be * the sonne of God.
Yea and the same dyd they that saw it when he
hong on the crosse, reproch hym with and obiect
agaynst hym . He * saued other (sayd they) hym
selfe he can not saue . Let hym now come downe
from the crosse & we will beleue hym . But now,
rising from the dead, to eternitie of lyfe, he declared a greater * power of hys Godhed, than if
in descendyng from the crosse he had fled from
the terrors of death . To dye * certainely is common to all : and though some for a tyme haue a-

uoyded

uoyded death intended agaynst them , yet to lose or breake the bondes of death ones suffered; and by hys owne power to rise alyue agayne, that is the proper doyng of the onely sonne of God Jesus Christ the author of lyfe , by which * he hath shewed hym selfe the conquerer of sinne and death yea and of the deuill hym selfe.

Rom.1.a.4.¶ 6.a.4.
¶.¶14.b.¶.
1.Cor.15.g.14.15.17.
Eph.1.b.20.
Col.1.c.17.18.
1.Joh.3.b.8.
Heb.2.b.14.

Ma. For what other cause rose he agayne?

Sch. That the prophecies of * Dauid and of other holy prophetes might be fulfilled , which told before , that neither hys bodie should be touched with corruption,nor his soule be left in hell,

Psal.16.b.10.
Mat.12.b.40.
Act.2.b.26.31.

Ma. But what profites bryngeth it vnto vs , that Christ rose agayne?

Sch. Manifold and diuerse.For therof commeth to vs * righteousnesse , which before we lacked: thense commeth to vs endeuour of * innocencie, which we call newnesse of lyfe : thense commeth to vs power,vertue, and strength to lyue well and holily : thense haue we hope that * our mortall bodies also shall one day be restored from death and rise whole agayne . For if Christ hym selfe had ben * destroyed by death , he had not bene our deliuerer . For what hope of safetie should we haue had left by hym that had not saued hym selfe ? It was therfore mete for the person which the Lord dyd beare , and a necessarie helpe for vs to saluation , that Christ should * first deliuer hym selfe from death , and afterward that he should breake.and pull in sonder the bandes of death for vs, ¶ so that we might set the hope of our saluation in his resurrection.For it can not be, * that Christ our head rising againe

Rom.4.b.25.

Rom.6.a.4.5.b.11.¶2.13.
Col.3.a.1-2.

Job.11.a.25.
Rom.8.b.11.
1.Cor.15.c.20 21.23.

1.Cor.15. c.13.14.16.
17.

Rom.8.b.11.
1.Cor.15.b.11.12.b.20.
21.
1.Pet.1.a.3.

Eph.1.b.22.¶ 4.c.
15.16.5.c.b.23.
Col.1.a.18.

should

ſhould ſuffer vs the members of hys bodie to be
conſumed and vtterly deſtroyed by death.

Ma. Thou haſt touched, my childe, the principall
cauſes of the reſurrection of Chriſt . Now would
I heare what thou thinkeſt of hys aſcending to
heauen.

Sch. He being couered with a cloud ſpred about
hym, in ſight of hys Apoſtles * aſcended into heauen, or rather aboue all heauens , where he ſitteth on the right hand of God the father.

Ma. Tell me how this is to be vnderſtoode?

Sch. Plainely, that Chriſt * in his bodie aſcended into heauen, where he had not afore bene in
hys bodie, and left the earth where he had afore
bene in hys bodie . For in hys nature of Godhed, which filleth all thinges, both he euer was
in heauen , and alſo with the ſame , and with
hys ſpirite, * he is alway preſent in earth with
hys Chirch, and ſhall be preſent till the end of
the world.

Ma. Then thou ſayeſt that there is one maner of
hys Godhed, and an other of hys Manhode.

Sch. Yea forſothe , maiſter . For we neither
make of hys Godhed a bo‾ie , nor of hys bodie
God. For hys Manhode is * a creature, hys Godhed not created. And the holy Scriptures wit-
neſſe that his * Manhode was taken vp into heauen , and abideth in heauen: but * hys Godhed
is ſo euery where, that it filleth both heauen and
earth .

Ma. But doeſt thou ſay that Chriſt is in any wiſe
preſent with vs in bodie.

Sch. If we may liken great thinges to ſmall,
Chriſtes bodie is ſo preſent to our faith , as the
L.j.   Sunne

Sunne when we see it, is present to our eye. For no one thing subiect to our senses commeth more nere to the likenesse of Christ, than the Sunne: which though it still abide in the heauen, and therefore in very deede toucheth not the eye, yet the bodie of the Sunne is present to the sight, notwithstanding so great a distance of place betwene. So the bodie of Christ, which by his ascending is taken vp from vs, *and hath left the world and is gone to hys father, is in deede absent from our senses: yet our fayth is *conuersant in heauen, & beholdeth that sonne of rightcousnesse, & is verily in presence with it there present, like as our sight is present with the bodie of the Sunne in the heauen, or as the Sunne is present with our sight in earth. Moreouer as the Sunne is with hys light present to all thinges, so is also Christ with hys Godhed, spirite, and power, *present to all and filleth all.

Joh.14.c.19.g 16.b. 16.b.30.

Act.7.g.55. Col.3.a.1. Heb.4.d.16.g 10.b.23 & 11.d.14.

Mat.28.b.20. 1.Cor.15.b.28. Eph.1.b.23. Col.1.c.17.18.

Ma. Now as touching Christ, what doest thou chiefely consider in his ascending and sitting at the right hand of his father?

Sch. It was mete, that Christ,* which from the hyest degree of honour and dignitie, had descended to the basest estate of a seruaunt, and to the reproche of condemnation and shamefull death, should on the other side obteine most noble glorie and excellent estate, euen the same which he had before, that hys glorie and maiestie might in proportion answere to hys basenesse and shame. Which thing S. Paule also writing to the Philippians, doth most plainely teach . *He became (sayth he) obedient vnto the death, euen the death of the Crosse. And therefore God made

Phil.2.a.6.7.8.

Phil.2.b.8.9.10. Eph.1.b.20.21.22.23. Col.3.c.1.d.18. Heb.2.b.9.

him

him the head of the Chirch, auaunced hym aboue
all principalities, endowed hym with the dominion of heauen and earth to gouerne all thinges,
exalted hym to the hyest heighth, and gaue hym
a name that is aboue all names, that at the name
of IESVS euery knee shoulde bowe, both of
thinges in heauen, earth, and hell.

Ma. When thou namest the right hand of God,
and sittyng, doest thou suppose and imagine that
God hath the shape or forme of a man?

Sch. No forsoth, maister. But bicause we speake
of God among men, we do in some sort after the
maner of men, expresse therby how Christ hath
receiued the kyngdome geuen hym of his father.
For*kynges vse to set thẽ on their right handsto
whom they vouchesaue to do hiest honor, & make
lieutenantes of their dominion. Therfore in these
wordes is meant that God the father * made
Christ his sonne the head of the Church, and that
by hym his pleasure is to preserue them that be
his, and to gouerne all thynges vniuersally.

Ma. Well sayd. Now what profite take we of hys
ascendyng into heauen, and sittyng on the right
hand of his father?

Sch. First Christ, as he had descended to the
earth, as into banishment, for our sake, so when
he went vp into heauen hys fathers inheritance,
he entred in our name, * makyng vs a way and
entrie thether, and openyng vs the gate of heauen which was before shut agaynst vs for sinne.
For sith Christ our hed hath caried with hym our
flesh into heauen, * he so mighty and louyng a
hed, will not leaue vs for euer in earth that are
members of hys bodie. Moreouer * he being pre-

L.ij.   sent

Margin notes:
1.Reg.5.c.tp
Psal.110.a.1.
Mat.20.c.26.

Eph.1.b.22.a 4.b
1r.16.a 5.a.27.
Col.1.b.18.

Joh.14.a.2.
2.Cor.5.a.1.
Ephe.2.b.18.
Heb.10.b.19.20.22.

Joh.17.b.24.
Eph.1.b.22.27.a 4.b
15.
Joh.16.b.26.
Rom.8.c.34.
Heb.7.b.25.6 9.a.24.
1.Joh.2.a.1.

ſent in the ſight of God, & commendyng vs vnto hym, and makyng interceſſion for vs, is the patrone of our cauſe, who beyng our aduocate our matter ſhall not quaile.

Ma. But why did he not rather tarry with vs here in earth?

Sch. When he had fully performed * all thynges that were appointed hym of hys father and which belonged to our ſaluation, he neded not to tarry any longer in earth. Yea alſo, all thoſe thynges he doth beyng abſent in bodie, which he ſhould do if he were bodily preſent, he preſerueth, comforteth and ſtrengthneth, correcteth, reſtraineth, & chaſteneth. Moreouer, as he promiſed, * he ſendeth down hys holy ſpirite from heauen into our hartes, as a moſt ſure pledge of hys good will, by which ſpirite he bringeth vs out of darkneſſe and myſt into open light, he geueth ſight to the blindeneſſe of our myndes, he chaceth ſorow out of our hartes and healeth the woundes therof, and with the * diuine motion of his ſpirite he cauſeth that lookyng vp to heauen we raiſe vp our mindes and hartes from the ground, from corrupt affections and from earthly thyngs vpward to the place where Chriſt is at the right hand of hys father, that we thinkyng vpon and beholdyng thynges aboue and heauenly, and ſo rayſed vp and of vpright minde we contemne theſe our baſe thynges, lyfe, death, richeſſe, pouertie, and with lofty and hye courage deſpiſe all worldly thinges. Finally this may be the ſumme, that Chriſt ſittyng on the right hand of God doth with his * power, wiſedome, and prouidence, rule and diſpoſe the world, moue, gouerne

and

and oꝛder all thynges, and so ſhall do, till the
frame of the woꝛld be diſſolued.

Ma. Sith then Chriſt beyng in his boꝛie taken vp
into heauen, doth yet not forſake hys here in earth,
they iudge very groſſely that meaſure his preſence
or abſence by hys bodie onely.

Sch. Pea truely. Foꝛ thynges that are not bo=
dily, can not be ſubiect to ſenſe. Who euer ſaw
his owne ſoule? No man. But what is pꝛeſen=
ter, what nerer, what cloſer ioyned, than eue=
ry mans ſoule to hym ſelfe? *Spirituall thynges
are not ſeen but with the eye of the ſpirit. Ther=
foꝛe who ſo will ſee Chꝛiſt in earth, let hym open
hys eyes, not of his bodie, but of hys ſoule and of
faith, and he ſhall ſee hym pꝛeſent whom the eye
ſeeth not.

Ma. But with whom doth faith acknowledge that
he is peculiarly and moſt effectually preſent?

Sch. The eye ſight of fayth ſhall eſpie hym pꝛe=
ſent, yea and in the middeſt, whereſoeuer *two
oꝛ thꝛee are gathered together in hys name: it
ſhall ſee hym pꝛeſent with them that be hys, that
is, with all the true godly, euen to the end of all
woꝛldes. What ſayd J? it ſhall ſee Chꝛiſt pꝛe=
ſent, yea euery godly perſon ſhall both ſee and
feele hym dwellyng in hym ſelfe, euen as hys
owne ſoule. Foꝛ he *dwelleth and abydeth
in that mans ſoule that ſetteth all hys truſt and
hope in hym.

Ma. Haſt thou yet any more to ſay hercof?

Sch. Chꝛiſt by aſcending and ſitting on the
right hand of hys father hath remoued, and
thꝛoughly rooted vp out of mens hartes *that
falſe opinion, which ſometyme hys *Apoſtles
           L.iij.   **them**

them selues had conceiued, namely that Christ
should reigne visible here in earth, as other
kynges of the earth and wordly princes do. The
° Joh.18.d.36. Lord would °pull this error out of our myndes,
and haue vs to thinke more hyely of hys kyng-
dome. Therfore hys will was to be absent from
our eyes and from all bodily sense, that by
this meane our °fayth may be both styrred vp
° Eph.1.d.18. and exercised to behold hys gouernance and pro-
Col.3.a.1.2. uidence that is not perceiued by bodily sense.

Ma. Is there any other reason why he withdrew
him selfe from the earth into heauen?

Sch. Sith he is prince not of some one land
°Mat.:8.d.18. °but of all landes of the world, yea and of °hea-
1.Cor.15.d.24.25.27.
28. uen also, and Lord both of quicke & dead, mete it
° Rom.14.b.9. was that he should gouerne his kyngdome in or-
Phil.2.b.9.10. der vnknowen to our senses. For if he should be
within the reach of sight, then must he nedes
change place & seate, and °be drawen now hether
° Luc.4.d.32.& 5.b now thether, and now & then remoue into sondry
contreys, to do hys affaires. For if in one mo-
ment of tyme he were euery where present with
all men, then should he seme not to be a man but
some ghost, and not to haue a verie bodie but
imaginatiue, or (as Eutyches thought) that his
bodie was turned into his Godhed, that it might
be thought to be euery where. Wherof would byandby arise infinite false opinions, all which he
hath dryuen away with carieng his bodie vp
whole into heauen, and hath deliuered mens
mindes from most foule errors. Yet in the meane
tyme, though he be not seen of vs, he wonderous-
° Mat.41.d.8. ly °ruleth and gouerneth the world, with most
Phil.1.b.9.10.
1 pet.1.b.15. hye power and wisedome. It is for men to gouerne

uerne and order their common weales after a
certaine order of men, but for Christ, that is, the
sonne of God, to do it after the maner of God.

Ma. Thou hast touched certaine of the chiefe of the
infinite, and vnmeasurable benefites, the fruite wherof we receaue by the death, resurrection, and ascension of Christ: for the whole can not be conceaued
by the minde & hart of man, much lesse in any wise
be expressed with wordes & vtterance. But yet thus
farre will I trye thy conning in thys matter, to haue
thee set me out briefely and in a summe the chiefe
principall pointes wherunto all the rest are referred.

Sch. Then I say, that both of these and of the
other doinges of Christ we take two kindes of
profite. The one, that what soeuer thinges he
hath done, he hath done them all for our benefite,
euen so farre as that they be * as much our owne,
so that with stedfast and liuely fayth we cleaue
vnto them, as if we our selues had done them.
He was crucified, and we also are crucified with
hym, and our sinnes punished in hym. He dyed
and was buried, we also together with our
sinnes are dead and buried, and that so as all the
remembrance of our sinnes is for euer forgotten.
He rose from death, and we also are risen againe
with hym, being so made partakers of hys resurrection and life, that from thence forth death
hath no more Dominion ouer vs.* For in vs is the
same spirite which raised Jesus Christ from the
dead. Finally, beside that since his ascension, we
haue most abundantly receaued the * giftes of
the holy Ghost, he hath also lifted and caried vs
vp into heauen with hym, that we might as it
were with our head, take possession therof. These

         L.iiij.   **thinges**

° Iob.2.b.11.
Rom.1.c.14.
1.Cor.1.b.30.
Col.1.a,5.d 2.a,3.5 3-
a.4.b.11.
1.Pet.1.c.4.

thinges in deede are not yet seen, *but then shall they be brought abrode into light, when Christ which is the light of the world, in whom all our hope and wealth is set and settled, shining with immortall glorie, shall shewe him selfe openly to all men.

Ma. What maner of profite is the other which we receaue of the doinges of Christ?

° Iob.13.b.15.
1.Pet.2.b.21.
1.Ioh.2.a.6.

Sch. That Christ hath set hymselfe for *an examplar for vs to follow, to frame our life according thereunto. Where Christ dyed for sinne, and was buried, he but once suffered the same. Where he rose againe and ascended into heauen, he but once rose againe, and but once ascended, he now dyeth no more, but enioyeth eternall life, and reigneth in most hye and euerlasting glorie. So

° Rom.6.a.2,3.c.10.
Gal.2.b.19.
Col.2.b.10.d 3.a.1.
2.Tim.2.b.11.

*if we be once dead & buried to sinne, how shall we hereafter liue in the same? If we be risen againe with Christ, if by assured fayth and stedfast hope we be conuersant with hym in heauen, then ought we from hence forth to bend all our cares and thoughtes vpon heauenly, diuine, and eternall thinges, not earthly, worldly, and transitorie. And as we haue *heretofore borne the

° Rom.8.f.20.
1.Cor.15.f.47.48.49.

image of the earthly man, we ought from hence forth to put on the image of the heauenly man, quietly and patiently bearing, after his example, all sorrowes and wronges, and following and expressing hys other diuine vertues so farre as mortall men be able. And whereas Christ our Lorde neuer ceasseth to do vs good, continually to entreate for and to craue hys fathers mercie for vs, to geue vs hys holy spirite, and wonderfully and continually to garnish his Chirch with

most

moſt liberall giftes, it is mete that *we in like
maner with our whole endeuour ſhould helpe
our neighbour, and that we be bound to all men
in moſt ſtreight bondes of loue, concozde, and
moſt nere frendſhip ſo much as ſhall lye in vs,
and ſo to be *wholly framed after the maners of
Chziſt as our onely examplar.

Ma. Are we not hereby alſo put in minde of our
dutie toward Chriſt?

Sch. We are in deede admoniſhed that we
*obey & follow the will of Chziſt, whoſe we are
wholly, and whom we pzofeſſe to be our Lozde:
that we ſo agayne on our part and with all our
affection loue, eſteme, & embzace Chziſt our Sauiour which ſhewed vs ſuch dere loue while we
were yet his enemies, as his moſt entier loue toward vs could not poſſibly be encreaſed: that we
hold Chziſt derer vnto vs than our ſelues: that to
Chziſt, which hath ſo geuen himſelfe wholly to
vs* we agayne yeld our ſelues wholly and all
that is ours: that we eſteme richeſſe, honozs, glory, our countrey, parentes, childzen, wyues, and
all dere pleaſant and delitefull thinges, of no value in compariſon of Chziſt, and accompt light
and deſpiſe all dangers foz Chziſt: finally that we
loſe our life and our very ſoule, rather than foz-
ſake Chziſt and our loue and dutie toward him.
foz happy is the death that being due to nature,
is chiefely yelded foz Chziſt, foz Chziſt I ſay,
which offred and yeelded him ſelfe to willing
death foz vs, and which being the authoz of life
both will and is able to *deliuer vs being dead
from death and to reſtoze vs to life.

Ma. Goe forward.

           M.j.   Sch.

Sch. We are furthermore taught , purely and sincerely to worship Christ the Lord now reigning in heauen, not with any * earthly worship, wicked traditions,and colde inuentions of men, but with heauenly and * very spirituall worship, such as may best beseme both vs that geue it and him that receiueth it, euen as he honored and honoreth his father , seing that all in one we geue the same honor to his father. For he that *honoreth Christ , honoreth also his father, whereof he him selfe is a most sure and substantiall witnesse.

Mat.15.a.5.6.8.9.
Joh.4.d.21.22.

Joh.4.c.23.24.

Joh.5.b.23.

Ma. Now I would heare thee tell me shortly what thou thinkest of the last Iudgement and of the end of the world.

Sch. Christ shall come * in the cloudes of the heauen , with most hye glory and with most honorable and reuerend maiesty , wayted on and besett with the company and multitude of holy Angels . And at the horrible sound, and dredfull blast of trumpet all the dead that haue liued from the creation of the world to that day,shall rise agayne with their soules and bodies whole and perfect , and shall * appere before his throne to be iudged , euery one for him selfe to geue accompt of their life,which shalbe examined by the vncorrupted and seuere iudge according to the truth.

Mat.24.c.29.30.6
2.c.11.
1.Cor.15.g.52.
1.Thef.4.b.16.

Rom.14.b.10.12.
1.Cor.4.a.4.5.
2.Cor.5.b.10.

Ma. But seing the day of iudgement shalbe in the end of the world, and death is lim'ted and certainely apointed for all, how doest thou in the Crede say that some shall then be quicke or aliue?

1.Cor.15.g.54.
1.Thef.4.c.17.

Sch. Saint Paul teacheth * that they which then shall remayne aliue, shall sodeinly be changed and made new , so that the* corruption of their bodies beyng taken away and mortalitie removed,

1.Cor.15.c.42.43.g.
53.54.
Phil.3.b.21.

remoued,they ſhall put on immoꝛtalitie,and this
change ſhalbe to them in ſtede of a death, becauſe
the endyng of coꝛrupted nature ſhalbe the begin-
nyng of a nature vncoꝛrupted.

Ma. Ought the godly at thinkyng vpon this iugement be ſtriken and abaſhed with feare,and to dread
it and ſhrinke from it?

Sch. No. Foꝛ he ſhall geue the ſentence, which
was once by the iudges ſentence condemned foꝛ
vs ,to the end that we commyng vnder the greuous iudgement of God ſhould not be condemned but acquited in iugement. He I ſay ſhall pꝛo-
nounce the iudgement in whoſe faith and pꝛotec-
tion we are, and which hath taken vpon hym
the defenſe of our cauſe. Yea 'our conſciences are
cherefully ſtayed with a moſt ſingular comfoꝛt,
and in the middes of the miſeries and woes of
this lyfe, do leape foꝛ ioy that Chꝛiſt ſhall one day
be the iudge of the woꝛld. Foꝛ vpon this hope we
chiefly reſt our ſelues , that then at laſt we ſhall
with vnchangeable eternitie poſſeſſe that ſame
kyngdome of immoꝛtalitie and euerlaſtyng lyfe,
in all partes fully and abundantly perfect which
hetherto' hath ben but begonne,and which was
oꝛdeined and appointed foꝛ the childꝛen of God
befoꝛe the foundations of the woꝛld were layd.
But the.' vngodly,which either haue not feared
the iuſtice and wꝛath of God , oꝛ haue not tru-
ſted in hys clementie and mercie by Chꝛiſt , and
which haue perſecuted the godly by land and
ſea, and done them all kyndes of wꝛong, and
ſlayne them with all ſoꝛtes of toꝛmentes and
moſt cruell deathes, ſhall with Sathan and all
the deuils be caſt into the pꝛiſon of hell appoin-

ted for them, the reuenger of their wickednesse and offenses, and into euerlastyng darkenesse, where beyng tormented with conscience of their owne sinnes, with eternall fire, and with all and most extreme execution, they shall pay and suffer eternall paines. For, that offense which mortall men haue done agaynst the vnmeasurable and infinite Maiestie of the immortall God, is worthy also of infinite and euerduryng punishment.

Ma. To the last iudgement is adioyned the end of the world, whereof I would haue thee speake yet more plainly.

Sch. The Apostle declareth that the end of the world shall be thus. The heauen shall passe away lyke a storme, the elementes with heate shalbe molten, the earth and all thynges in it shalbe inflamed with fire, as if he should say, the tyme shall come when this world burnyng with heate, all the corruption therof (as we see in gold) tried out by fire, shall be wholly fyned, and renewed to most absolute and hye perfection, and shall put on a most beautifull face which in euerlastyng ages of worldes shall neuer be changed. For this is it that Saint Peter sayth, we looke for, accordyng to the promise of God, a new heauen and a new earth, wherin righteousnesse shall inhabite. Neither is it vncredible, that as sinne, so the corruption of thynges, and changeablenesse, and other euilles growen of sinne, shall once at the last haue an end. And this is the summe of the second part of the Christian fayth, wherein is conteined the whole storie of our redemption by Jesus Christ.

Ma. Sithe then thou hast now spoken of God the father

Mat.24.c.29.30.&31.
2.Pet.3.c.10.11.&c.

2.Pet.3.c.4.

Rom.8.c.19.22.&c.
2.Pet.3.c.13.
Apoc.21.a.1.

Conclusion.

father the creator, and of his sonne Iesus Christ the
Sauiour, and so hast ended two partes of the Christian confession, now I would heare thee speake of
the third part , what thou beleuest of the H O L Y
GHOST.

The third part
of the Crede.
The Holy
Ghost.

Sch. I confesse that he is the ⋅ third person of the
most holy Trinitie , proceding from the father
& the sonne before all beginning, egall with them
both , & of the very same substance, and together
with them both to be honored and called vpon.

° Mat.28.b.19.
Joh.14.b.26.& 15.b.
16.& 16.b.7.& 20.&&c
&c.3.a.3.4.

Ma. Why is he called Holy?

Sch. Not onely for his owne holinesse, which
yet is the hyest holynesse, but also for that by hym
the elect of God and ⋅ the members of Christ are
made holy. For which cause the holy Scriptures
haue called hym the spirite of sanctification.

° Rom.1.b.4.& 15.b.
16.
2.Thess.2.c.13.
Tit.3.b.5.
1.Pet.1.a.2.

Ma. In what thynges doest thou thinke that this
sanctification consisteth?

Sch. First we are by his instinct and breathyng
⋅ newly begotten, and therfore Christ sayd that
we must be borne agayne of water and the spirit. Also by hys heauenly breathyng on vs, God
the father doth ⋅ adopt vs his children, & therfore
he is worthily called the spirit of adoption . By
his expoundyng, the ⋅ diuine mysteries are opened vnto vs. By his light, the eyes of our soules
are made clere to vnderstand them. By his iugement, sinnes ⋅ are either pardoned or reserued. By
his strength, ⋅ sinfull flesh is subdued and tamed,
and corrupt desires are bridled & restrained . It
his will, ⋅ manifold giftes are distributed among
the godly . Finally, by hys power, our mortall
bodies ⋅ shall rise alyue agayne. Briefly, what soeuer benefites are geuen vs in Christ, all these

° Joh.3.a.3.
Tit.3.b.5.

° Rom.8.c.15.&&c
Gal.4.a.5.6.

° Joh.14.b.17.b.26.
& 16.b.13.
1.Cor.2.c.10.11.b.&c
Eph.1.b.17.

° Joh.20.c.22.

° Rom.7.a.4.5.& 8.b.
13.14.& c.26.26.

° Act.2.a.4.
1.Cor.12.d.4.7.& c

° Rom.8.b.11.

M.iij.   ⋅ we

* L.Cq.12.2.4.7.4¢.

" we vnderſtand, feele, and receaue by the worke of the holy ghoſt. Not vnworthily therfore we put confidence and truſt in the author of ſo great giftes, and do worſhyp and call vppon hym.

The iiij part of the Crede.

The Chirch.

Ma. Now remaineth the fowerth part, of T H E HOLY CATHOLIKE CHIRCH, of the which I would heare what thou thinkeſt.

Sch. I will bryng into few wordes, that which the holy Scriptures do hereof largely and plentifully declare. Before that the Lord God made heauen and earth, he determined to haue to hym ſelfe a certaine moſt beautifull kyngdome and moſt holy common weale. This the Apoſtles that wrote in Greke, called *Ecclesia*, which by interpretyng the word, may fittly be called, a *Congregation*. Into this, as into hys owne citie, God did incorporate an ˙ infinite multitude of men, which muſt all be ſubiect, ſeruiſable and ˙ obedient to Chriſt their onely kyng, and which haue all committed them ſelues to hys protection, and of whom he hath taken vpon hym to be defender, and doth continually mainteine and preſerue them. To this common weale do all they properly belong, ˙ as many as truely feare, honor, ⁊ call vpon God, altogether applying their myndes to liue holily, and godly, and which puttyng all their truſt and hope in God do moſt aſſuredly looke for the bleſſedneſſe of eternall lyfe. They that be ſtedfaſt, ſtable, and conſtant in this fayth, * were choſen and appointed, and (as we terme it) predeſtinated to this ſo great felicitie, before the foundations of the world were layed. whereof they haue a

˙ Mat.16.t.18.

˙ Mat.18.b.19. Act.2.a.5.9. 2.Cor.12.b.13.

˙ Ephe.5.d.27.24.

˙ Act.10.d.34.35. Rom.2.b.11. Gal.5.b.17.16. Col.3.b.12.13.16.

˙ Mat.16.c.18. Rom.8.c.30.30. Ephe.1.a.4.5. 2.⸺1.b.12. Eſa.1. a.1.

*wit⸗

* witnesse within them in their soules the spirite
of Christ the author and therewith also the
most sure pledge of this confidence . By the instinct of which diuine spirite , I do also most
surely persuade my selfe that I am also by Gods
good gift through Christ freely made one of this
blessed citie.

Ma. It is sure a godly and very necessary persuasion.
Now therfore geue me the definition of the Church
that thou speakest of.

Sch. I may most briefely & truely say, that * THE
CHIRCH IS THE BODY OF CHRIST.

Ma. Yea but I would haue it somewhat more plainly and at large.

Sch. The Church is * the body of the Christian
common weale, that is, the vniuersall number
and fellowship of all the faithfull , whom God
through Christ hath before all beginning of time
* apointed to euerlasting life.

Ma. Why is this point put into the Crede?

Sch. Bicause if the Church were not, both Christ
had dyed without cause, and all the thinges that
haue bene hetherto spoken of, should be in vaine
and come to nothing.

Ma. How so?

Sch. Bicause hetherto we haue spoken of the
causes of saluation, & haue considered the foundations therof, namely, how God by the deseruing
of Christ loueth vs and derely esteemeth vs, how
also by the worke of the holy Ghost we receiue
this grace of God whereunto we are restored.
But of these this is the onely effect, *that there
be a Chirch, that is, a company of the godly vpon
whom these benefites of God may be bestow-

M.iiij.   ed,

ed,that there be a certayne blessed citie and common weale , in which we ought to lay vp and as it were to consecrate all that we haue, and to geue our selues wholly vnto it,and for which we ought not to sticke to dye.

Ma. Why doest thou call this Chirch holy?

Sch. That by this marke it may be * discerned from the wicked company of the vngodly . For all those whom God hath chosen,he hath restored vnto holinesse of life and innocencie.

Ma. Is this holinesse which thou doest attribute to the chirch , alredy vpright and in all pointes perfect?

Sch. Not yet . For so long as we liue à mortall life in this world , such is the * feblenesse ﬤ frailtie of mankinde , we are of to weake strength wholly to shunne all kindes of vices.Therefore the holinesse of the Chirch is not yet full and perfectly finished, but yet very well begonne . But when it shall be fully ioyned to Chriſt , from * whom she hath all her cleannesse and purenesse, then shall she be clothed with innocencie and holinesse in all pointes full and perfectly finished, as with à certayne snowywhite and most pure garment.

Ma. To what purpose doest thou call this Chirch Catholike?

Sch. It is as much as if J called it vniuersall. For this company or assembly of the godly is not pent vp in any certayne place or time, but it conteineth and comprifeth the vniuersall number of the faythfull , that haue liued and shall liue in all places and ages since the beginning of the worlde , that there may be one body of the

Chirch,

Chirch, *as there is one Christ, the onely head of the body . For whereas the Iewes claimed and chalenged to them selues the Chirch of God as peculiar and by lineall right due to their nation, and sayd that it was theirs, and helde it to be onely theirs: the Christian fayth professeth that a *great number and infinite multitude of godly persons, gathered together out of all countreyes of the world, out of all partes of all nations euery where, and all ages of all times, by the strength and power of his holy worde and voice, and by the diuine motion of his heauenly spirite, is by God incorporated into this Chirch as into his owne citie, which all agreing together in one * true fayth, one minde and voice, may be in all thinges obedient to Christ their onely king, as members* to their head.

Ma. Doest thou thinke that they do well that ioyne to this part of the Christian beliefe, that they beleue the holy catholike Chirch of Rome?

Sch. I do not onely thinke that they ioyne à wrong forged sense to this place, while they will haue no man to be compted in the Chirch of Christ but him that esteemeth for holy all the Decrees and ordinances of the Bishop of Rome, but also I iudge that when by adding afterward the name of one nation they abridge and drawe into narrowe roome the vniuersall extent of the Chirch, which them selues do first confesse to be farre and wide spred abrode euery where among all landes and peoples, they are herein farre madder then the Iewes, ioyning and pronouncing with one breath mere contrary sayinges. But into thys madnesse are they driuen by à

    blinde

blinde gredinesse, and desire, to shift and foyst in
the Bishop of Rome to be head of the Chirch in
earth, in the stede of Christ.

Ma. Now woulde I heare thee tell, why after the
holy Chirch, thou immediatly addest, that we beleue THE COMMVNION OF SAINTES.

Sch. Because these two belong all to one thing,
and are very fitly matched and agreeing together. For this parcell doth somwhat more plainly expresse the conioyning and societie that is
among the members of the Chirch, than which
there can none be nerer. For whereas God hath
as well in all coastes and countreyes, as in all
times and ages, them that worship him purely
and sincerely,* all they, though they be seuered
and sondred by diuerse and farre distant times
and places, in what nation soeuer, or in what
land soeuer they be, are yet members most nerely
conioyned and knitte together of one and of the
selfe same bodie wherof Christ is the head. Such
is the communion that the godly haue with God
and among them selues. * For they are most
nerely knitte together in communitie of spirite,
of fayth, of sacramentes, of prayers, of forgeuenesse of sinnes, of eternall felicitie, and finally, of
all the benefites that God geueth hys Chirch
through Christ. Yea they are so ioyned together
with most straight bondes of concord * and loue,
they haue so all one minde, that the profite of any
one and of them all is all one, and to this endeuour they do most bend them selues, how they
may with enterchaunge of beneficiall doinges
with counsell and helpe further eche other, in all
thinges, and specially to atteyning of that blessed

and

and eternall life. But bicause this communion of
saintes can not be perceaued by our senses, nor by
any * naturall kinde of knowledge or force of vnderstanding, as other ciuile communities & fel-
lowships of men may be, therfore it is here rightly placed among these thinges that lye in beleife.

Ma. I like very well this briefe discourse of the
Church, and of the benefites of God bestowed vpon
her through Christ : For the same is most plainly
taught in the holy Scriptures. But may the Chirch
be otherwise knowen, than by beleuing by fayth.

Sch. Here in the Crede is properly entreated of
the congregation of those whom God by hys secret * election hath adopted to him selfe through
Christ: which Chirch can neither be seen with
eyes, nor can continually be knowen by signes.
Yet there is a Chirch of God visible or that may
be seen, the tokens or markes whereof he doth
shewe and open vnto vs.

Ma. Than that this whole matter of the Chirch
may be made plainer, so describe and paint me out
that same visible Chirch with her markes and signes
that it may be discerned from any other fellowship
of men.

Sch. I will assay to do it as well as I can. The
visible Chirch is nothing els but a certaine multitude of men, which, in what place soeuer they
be, * do professe the doctrine of Christ pure and
syncere, euen the same which the Euangelistes
and Apostles haue in the euerlasting monu-
mentes of holy Scriptures faythfully disclosed
to memorie, and which do truely call vpon God
the father * in the name of Christ, and moreouer
do vse hys * mysteries, commonly called Sacra-

N.ij.   mentes,

mentes, with the same purenesse and simplicitie (as touching their substance) which the Apostles of Christ vsed and haue put in writing.

Ma. Thou sayest then that the markes of the visible Chirch are, the syncere preaching of the Gospell, that is to say, of the benefites of Christ, inuocation, and administration of the sacramentes.

Sch. These are in deede the chiefe, and the necessarie markes of the visible Chirch, such as without the which it can not be in dede nor rightly be called the Chirch of Christ . But yet also in the same Chirch, if it be well ordered, there shall be seen to be obserued a certaine * order and maner of gouernance, and such a forme of ecclesiasticall Discipline, that it shall not be free for any that abideth in that flocke, publikely to speake or do any thing wickedly or in hainous sort, without punishment, yea and so, that in that congregation of men, all offences (so farre as is possible) be auoyded . But this discipline since long tyme past by litle and litle decaying, as the maners of men be corrupt and out of right course, specially of the riche and men of power, which will nedes haue impunitie and most free libertie to sinne and do wickedly, this graue maner of looking to them and of chastisement can hardly be mainteined in Chirches . But in what soeuer assemblie , the worde of God, the calling vpon hym, and his sacramentes, are purely and syncerely reteined, it is no doubt that there is also the Chirch of Christ.

Ma. Are not then all they that be in thys visible Chirch, of the number of the electe to euerlasting life ?

* Mat. 18.c.15.16.17.
1.Cor.4.b.21.3 10.g.
11.32. g 14.e 26.g.40.
Phi.2.b.14.11.
1. Thess.c.14.b.22.
g 2.Thess.3.b.14.15.
Col.2.a.5.
1.Tim.2.c.8.9. &
g 5.a.1.2.
Tit.2.a.2.3.4. &
g.1.c.10.

Sch. Many by hypocrisie and counterfaiting of godlinesse do ioyne them selues to this fellow∫hip, which are nothing lesse than true members of the Chirch . But forasmuch as where soeuer the worde of God is ∫yncerely taught, and his facramentes rightly mini∫tred , there are euer some appointed to*saluation by Chri∫t, we compt all that whole companie to be the Chirch of God, ∫eing that Chri∫t also promi∫eth that him ∫elf will be pre∫ent with two * or three that be gathered together in hys name.

Ma. Why doe∫t thou byandby after the Chirch, make mention of the forgeuene∫∫e of ∫innes.

Sch. Fir∫t becau∫e the * keyes , wherewith hea∫uen is to be ∫hut and opened, that is, that power of binding and loo∫ing, of re∫eruing and forge∫uing ∫innes, which ∫tandeth in the mini∫terie of the worde of God, is by Chri∫t geuen and com∫mitted to the Chirch, and properly belongeth vn∫to the Chirch . Secondly, bicau∫e no man obtei∫neth forgeuene∫∫e of ∫innes , that is not à true member of the body * of Chri∫t, that is, ∫uch à one as doth not earne∫tly , godlily , holily , yea and continuingly *and to the end embrace and main∫teine the common fellow∫hip of the Chirch.

Ma. Is there then no hope of saluation out of the Chirch?

Sch. Out of it can be nothing but damnation, death, and de∫truction . For what hope of life can remaine * to the members when they are pulled a∫under and cut off from the head and bo∫die . They therefore that ∫editiou∫ly ∫tirre vp di∫∫corde * in the Chirch of God , and make diui∫ion and ∫trife in it, and trouble it with ∫ectes, haue all
hope

hope of safetie by forgeuenesse of sinnes cut of from them till they be reconciled and returne to agreement and fauour with the Chirch.

Ma. What meanest thou by thys worde Forgeuenesse?

Sch. That the faythfull do obteine at Gods hand discharge of their fault, and pardon of their offense: for God * for Christes sake freely forgeueth them their sinnes, and rescueth and deliuereth them from iudgement and damnation, and from punishmentes iuste and due for their ill doing.

Ma. Can not we then with godly dutiefull doinges and workes satisfie God, and by our selues merite pardon of our sinnes?

Sch. There is no mercie due to our merites, but God doth yeld and remitte to Christ hys correction and punishment that he would haue done vpon vs. For Christ alone, with sufferance of hys paines, * and with hys death, wherwith he hath payed and performed the penaltie of our sinnes, hath satisfied God. Therfore by Christ alone we haue accesse to the grace of God. We receauing thys benefite of * hys free liberalitie & goodnesse, haue nothing at all to offer or render agayne to hym by way of reward or recompense.

Ma. Is there nothing at all to be done on our behalfe, that we may obteine forgeuenesse of sinnes?

Sch. Although among men, the fault once graunted, it is hard to obteine forgeuenesse of hym that ought to be the punisher of offenses, yet euen they * that are strangers to our religion, haue not bene ignorant, that confession is a certaine remedie to hym that hath done amisse. And I haue already sayd how sinners for obteyning of pardon

* Psal.17.a.c.?.
Act.13.f.3?.5. & 26.D.18.
Rom 3.D.24.
Eph.1.b.7.
Col.1.c.13.14.

* Esa.17.a.4.?.b.2.b.
12.
Rom.c.b.3.10.
Col.1.c.20.21.
2.Tim.1.c.10.
Heb.9.D.14-15.

* Rom.1.b.24-25.27.
31.
Gal.2.c.16.

pardon haue neede of repentance, which some
like better to call Resipiscence, oz amendment,
and of change of minde : and the Lozd pzomiseth
that he will pardon sinners if they repent, * if
they amend and turne their hartes from their
naughtie liues vnto hym.

Ma. How many partes be there of Repentance?

Sch. Two cheife partes . The moztifying of the
olde man oz the flesshe : and the quickening of the
new man oz the spirite.

Ma. I woulde haue these more largely and plainly set out.

Sch. The moztifying of the olde man is vnfay-
ned and syncere acknowledging and * confession
of sinne, and therewith ā shame and sozrowe of
minde, with the feling whereof the person is soze
greued foz that he hath swarued from righteousnesse and not bene obedient to the will of God.
Foz euery man ought, in remembzing the sinnes
of hys life passed, wholly to * mislike him selfe, to
be angry with him selfe, and to be a seuere iudge
of hys owne faultes, and to geue sentence and
pzonounce iudgement of him selfe, to the intent
he abide not the greuous iudgement of God in
hys wzath. Thys sozrowe some haue called Con-
trition, whereunto are ioyned in nerenesse and
nature an earnest hatred of sinne, and a loue and
desire of righteousnesse lost.

Ma. But the conscience of hainous offenses , & the
force of repentance may be so great that the minde
of man on eche side compassed with feare may be
possessed with despeire of saluation,

Sch. * That is true, vnlesse God bzing comfozt to
the greatnesse of sozrow . But to the godly there

     remaineth

* Eph. 4. d. 23. 24.
1. Pet. 4. b. 6.

remaineth yet one other part of repentance, which is called * Renuing of the spirite, or quickning of the new man. That is, when fayth commeth and * refresheth and lifteth vp the minde so troubled, asswageth sorrowe, and comforteth the person, and doth reuoke & raise him vp againe from desperation, to hope of obteyning pardon of God through Christ, & from the gate of death, yea from hell it selfe vnto life. And this is it that we professe that we beleue the Forgeuenesse of sinnes.

* Math. 4. c. 17.
Luk. 4. f. 38. g. 42. 43.
44. and 11. d. 13. 21. and
15. c. 21. and 14. f. 47.
Act. 7. c. f. 37. and. 3. b.
10. and. 16. f. 30. 31.
1. Tim. 1. c. 15.

Ma. Is man able in this feare & these hard distresses to deliuer him selfe by hys owne strength?

* Math. 19. b. 16.
Luk. 15. c. 22.
2. Cor. 4. a. 3. 4.
2. Chron. 2. b. 16. 17.

Sch. Nothyng lesse. For it is onely God * which strengtheneth man despeiring of hys own estate, rayseth him vp in affliction, restoreth him in vtter miserie, and by whose guiding the sinner conceaueth this hope, minde, and will that I spake of.

Ma. Now rehearse the rest of the Crede.

* Math. 22. d. 31. 32.
Iob. 11. c. 21.
1. Cor. 15. total.

Sch. I beleue THE RESVRRECTION OF THE FLESH, *AND LIFE EVERLASTING.

Ma. Bicause thou hast touched somewhat of thys before in speaking of the last iudgement, I will aske thee but a fewe questions. Whereto or why do we beleue these thinges.

* 1. Cor. 15. d. 14. 18.
19. 19.

Sch. Although we beleue that the soules of men are immortall and euerlasting, yet if we should thinke that our bodies should by death be vtterly destroyed for euer, then must we nedes be* wholly discouraged, for that wanting the one part of our selues, we should neuer entierly possesse perfecte ioye and immortalitie. We do therfore certainly beleue, not only that our soules, when we depart out of this life, being deliuered from the company
of

of our bodies, do byandby flye vp pure & whole
* into heauen to Chꝛist, but also that our bodies
shall at length be restoꝛed *to a better state of life,
and ioyned againe to their soules, and so we shall
wholly be made perfectly and fully blessed, that
is to say, we dout not that both in our bodyes
and soules we shall enioy eternitie, immoꝛtalitie,
and most blessed life, that shall neuer in euerla=
sting continuance of time be changed . Thys
hope * comfoꝛteth vs in miseries . Endued with
thys hope, we not onely patiently suffer and
beare the incommodities and combꝛances that
light vpon vs in this life, but also very departure
from life and the soꝛrowes of death . Foꝛ we are
thꝛoughly perswaded that death is not a de=
struction that endeth and consumeth all thinges,
but a guide foꝛ vs to heauen that setteth vs in
the way of a quiet, easie, blessed, and euerlasting
life . And therefoꝛe gladly & cherefully we runne,
yea we flye out, from the bondes of our bodyes
as from a pꝛison, to heauen as to the common
towne and citie of God and men.

Ma. Doth the beleuing of these thinges auaile vs
to any other end?

Sch. We are put in minde, that we comber not
noꝛ entangle our selues with vncertaine, transi=
toꝛie, and fraile thinges : that we bend not our
eye to earthly gloꝛie and felicitie : but inhabite
thys woꝛld * as strangers, and euer minding our
remouing : that we long vpward foꝛ heauen and
heauenly thinges, where we shall in blisse enioye
eternall life .

Ma. Sithe thou hast before sayd, that the wicked
shall rise againe, in sort most farre *differing from the

godly, that is to say, to eternall miserie and euerlasting death, why doth the Crede make mention only of life euerlasting, and of hell no mention at all?

Sch. Thys is a confession of the Christian fayth,
which perteineth to none but to the godly, and
therefore rehearseth onely those thinges that are
* fitt for to comfort, namely the most large giftes
which God will geue to them that be hys . And
therefore here is not recited what punishmentes
are prouided for them that be out of the kingdome of God.

Ma. Now thou hast declared the Crede, that is, the
summe of the Christian fayth, tell me, what profite
get we of this fayth?

Sch. Rightcousnesse * before God , by which we
are made heires of eternall life.

Ma. Doth not then our owne godlinesse toward
God , and leading of our life honestly and holily
among men, iustifie vs before God?

Sch. Of thys we haue sayd somewhat already
after the declaring of the law , & in other places,
to thys effect . If any man were able to liue vprightly according to the precise rule * of the law
of God, he should worthily be compted iustified
by hys good workes. But seing we are * all most
farre from that perfection of life, yea and be so
oppressed with conscience of our sinnes, we *must
take an other course, and finde an other way,
how God may receaue vs into fauour , than by
our owne deseruing.

Ma. What way?

Sch. We must flee to the * mercie of God, wherby he freely embraceth vs with loue & good will,
in Christ, without any our deseruing, or respect of
workes,

* Mar.16.b.16.
Luc.24.c.47.
Ioh.1.c.11.16.
Rom.4.c.16.

* Rom.3.c.21.22.
Gal.2.b.16.

* Rom.10.a.5.
Gal.3.b.12.

* Gen.6.b.c.9 8.b.11.
Luc.18.c.11.12.14.
Rom.−.c.14-17.
Gal.2.c.16.

* Rom.11.a.6.

* Rom.1.c.24.and 4.
a.a.* b.16.
Ephe.1.a.4.5.
2 Tim.1.b.9.
Tit.3.b.4.5.
1.Pet.1.a.3. & 2.b.10.

workes, both forgeuing vs our sinnes, and so geuing vs the righteousnesse of Christ by fayth in
him, that for the same Christes righteousnesse he
so accepteth vs, as if it were our owne. To Gods
mercie therefore through Christ we ought to im-
pute all our iustification.

Ma. How do we know it to be thus?

Sch. By the Gospell, which conteineth the promises of God by Christ, * to the which when we
adioyne fayth, that is to say, an assured perswa-
sion of minde, and stedfast confidence of Gods
good will, such as hath bene set out in the whole
Crede, we do as it were take state and possession
of thys Iustification that I speake of.

Ma. Doest thou not then say, that fayth is the
principall cause of thys iustification, so as by the
merite of fayth we are compted righteous before
God?

Sch. No: for that were to set fayth in the place
of Christ. But the springhead of thys iustification
* is the mercie of God, which is conueyed to vs
by Christ, and is offred to vs by the Gospell,
*and receaued of vs by fayth as with a hand.

Ma. Thou sayest then, that faith is not the cause but
the Instrument of iustification, for that it embraceth
Christ * which is our iustification, coupling vs with
so straight bond to hym that it maketh vs partakers
of all hys good thinges.

Sch. Yea forsooth.

Ma. But can thys iustification be so seuered from
good workes, that he that hath it can want them?

Sch. No: for by fayth we receaue Christ such
as he deliuereth hym selfe vnto vs. But he doth
not onely set vs at libertie from sinnes and

            D.ij.   death,

*Rom.4.a.5.7.d.14.
16.b.20.24.
Gal.2.c.16.d.20.and
3.b.11.
Heb.10.g.38.

*Ephe.1.a.4.5.6.gd.
and 2.d.4.5.
Tit.3.b.4.5.6.

* Mat.1.b.14-15.
Rom.4.c.16.b.19.20.
21.24.

* Joh.1.a.12.
Rom.3.b.22.
1.Cor.1.b.30.
Heb.9.b.14.

death, and make vs at one with God, but also with the diuine inspiration and vertue of the * Holy Ghost doth regenerate and newly forme vs to the endeuour of innocencie and holinesse, which we call * newnesse of life.

Ma. Thou sayest then, that * Iustice, faith, & good workes, do naturally cleaue together, and therefore ought no more to be seuered, than Christ the author of them in vs can be seuered from him selfe.

Sch. It is true.

Ma. Then thys doctrine of fayth doth not with-drawe mens mindes from godly workes and duties.

Sch. Nothyng lesse. For good workes do stand vppon fayth as * vppon their roote. So farre therfore is fayth from withdrawing our hartes from liuing vprightly, that contrariwyse it doth most vehemently stirre vs vp to the endeuour of good life, yea and so farre that he is not truely faythfull that doth not also to his power, both * shunne vices and embrace vertues, so liuing alwayes, as one that looketh to geue an accompt.

Ma. Therefore tell me plainly, how our workes be acceptable to God, and what rewardes be geuen to them.

Sch. In good workes two thynges are princi-pally required. First that we do those workes * that are prescribed by the law of God, secondly that they be done with that minde and * fayth which God requireth. For no doinges, or thoughtes, enterprised or * conceaued without fayth, can please God.

Ma. Goe forward.

Sch. It is euident therefore that all workes what

what ſoeuer we do befoze that we * be bozne agayne and renued by the ſpirite of God, ſuch as may propperly be called our owne wozkes, are faultie. Foz what ſoeuer ſhewe of gayneſſe and wozthineſſe they repzeſent and geue to the eyes of men, ſithe they ſpzing and procede from à faulty and cozrupted * hart which God chiefely conſidereth, they can not but be defiled and cozrupted, and ſo greuouſly offend God. Such wozkes therefoze, as euill fruites * growing out of an euill tree, God deſpiſeth and reiecteth from hym.

Ma. Can we not therefore preuent God with any workes or deſeruinges, whereby we may firſt prouoke hym to loue vs and be good vnto vs?

Sch. Surely with none. Foz God loued and choſe vs in Chzift, not onely when we were hys enemies, * that is, ſinners, but alſo befoze the foundations of the wozld were layed. And this is the ſame ſpzinghead and oziginall of our iuſtification, whereof J ſpake befoze.

Ma. What thinkeſt thou of thoſe workes, which we after that we be reconciled to Gods fauour, do by the inſtinct of the Holy Ghoſt?

Sch. The dutiefull wozkes of godlineſſe, which procede out of fayth wozking * by charitie, are in dede acceptable to God, yet not by their owne deſeruing, * but foz that he of hys liberalitie vouchſaueth them hys fauour. Foz though they be deriued from the ſpzite of God, as little ſtreames from the ſpzing head, yet of our * fleſh, that mingleth it ſelfe with them in the doing by the way, they receaue cozruption, as it were by infection, like as a riuer, otherwiſe pure and

D.iij. clere,

clere, is troubled and mudded with mire and slyme wherethrough it runneth.

Ma. How then doest thou say that they please God?

* Rom.9.f.31.32.
Gal.1.a.6.
Heb.11.b.6.

* Psal.130.a.3.and 143.a.2.

Sch. * It is fayth that procureth Gods fauour to our workes, while it is assured that he will not deale with vs after extremitie of * lawe, nor call our doinges to exacte accompt, nor trie them as it were by the squire, that is, he will not in valuing and weying them vse seueritie, but remitting and pardonyng all their corruptnesse, for Christes sake and hys deseruinges, will accompt them for fully perfect.

Ma. Then thou standest still in thys, that we can not by merite of workes obteyne to be iustified before God, seing thou thinkest that all doinges of men, euen the perfectest do nede pardon.

* Luk.18.c.11.12.14.
Rom.3 a.2.
Gal.2.c.16.

*.Rom.2.c.10.

* Psal.143.a.2.

* Job.4.b.18.and 15.b.14.15.16.and 25.b.4.5.6.
Psal.130.a.3.

* Job.11.b.14.15.16.
pro.20.b.6.
Esa.64.b.6.
1 Cor.4.a.4.

Sch. God hym selfe hath so decreed in hys word, and hys holy spirite doth teach vs to pray that he * bring vs not into iudgement. For where rightcousnesse, such as God the iudge shall allowe, ought to be throughly * absolute, and in all partes and pointes fully perfect, such as is to be directed and tried by the most precise rule, and as it were by the plumme line of Gods lawe and iudgement: and sithe our workes, euen * the best of them, for that they swarue and differ most farre from the rule and prescription of Gods lawe and iustice, are many wayes to be blamed and condemned: we can in no wise be iustified before God by workes.

Ma. Doth not thys doctrine withdrawe mens mindes from the duties of godlinesse, and make them slacker and slower to good workes, or at least

lesse

lesse cherefull and ready to godly endeuours?

Sch. No. For we may not therefore say that good workes are vnprofitable or done in vayne and without cause, for that we obteine not iustification by them. For they serue both to the profite of our neighbour * and to the glorie of God, and they do as by certaine testimonies * assure vs of Gods good will toward vs, and of our loue againe to God ward, and of our fayth, and so consequently of our saluation. And reason it is, that we being redemed with the bloud of Christ the sonne of God, and hauyng beside receaued innumerable and infinite benefites of God, should liue and wholly frame our selues after the * will and appointment of our redemer, and so shewe our selues mindefull and thankfull to the author of our saluation, and * by our example procure and winne other vnto hym. The man that calleth these thoughtes to mynde, may sufficiently reioyce in hys good endeuours and workes.

Ma. But God doth allure vs to good doing with certaine rewardes, both in this life and in the life to come, and doth couenaunt with vs as it were for certaine wages.

Sch. * That reward, as I haue sayd, is not geuen to workes for their worthinesse, and rendred to them as recompense for deseruinges, but by the bountifullnesse of God, is freely bestowed vpon vs without deseruing. And iustification God doth geue vs as a gift of hys owne deare loue toward vs and of hys liberalitie * through Christ. When I speake of Gods gift and liberalitie, I meane it * free and bountifull without

D.iiij.　　any

any our deſert or merite: that it be Gods mere
and ſyncere liberalitie, which he applyeth to our
ſaluation onely whom he loueth and which truſt
in hym, not hyered, or procured for wages, as it
were à marchandiſe of hys commodities and be-
neſites vſed by hym for ſome profite to hym ſelfe,
requiring agayne of vs ſome recompenſe or price:
which once to thinke, were to abate both the liberalitie and maieſtic of God.

Ma. Whereas then God doth by fayth both geue
vs iuſtification, and by the ſame fayth alloweth and
accepteth our workes, tell me, doeſt thou thinke
that this fayth is a qualitie of nature, or the gift
of God?

Sch. Fayth is the gift * of God, and a ſingular
and excellent gift. For both our wittes are to
groſſe * and dull to conceaue and vnderſtand the
wiſedome of God, whoſe fountaines are opened
by fayth, and our hartes are more apt either
* to diſtruſt, or to wrongfull and corrupt truſt in
our ſelues, or in other creatures, than to true
truſt in God. But God inſtructing vs with hys
worde, and * lightening our mindes with hys
holy ſpirit, maketh vs apt to learne thoſe thinges
that otherwiſe would be farre from entring into
the dull capacitie of our wittes, and ſealing the
promiſes of ſaluation in our ſoules, he ſo infor-
meth vs that we are moſt ſurely perſwaded of
the truth of them. Theſe thynges the Apoſtles
vnderſtanding, do pray to the Lord to * encreaſe
their fayth.

* Mar. 1.c.23.24.
Job.6.c.29.
1.Pet.1.b.10.11.

* Mat.16.b.7.&.9.11.
Luk.18.f.34.
Rom.8.b.6.7.
1.Cor.2.b.14.

* Marh.6.b.30.and
8.c.26.and.16.b.8.
and 14.b.31.

* Mat.16.c.17.
Luk.24.g.45.
Col.1.b.9.
2.Tim.2.&.7.

* Luk.17.a.c.

¶ *The*

¶ The third part.

Of Prayer, and Thankesgeuing.

Ma. Thou haſt in good time made mention of Prayer. For now thou haſt ended the declaration of the Law of God, and of the Crede, that is to ſay, the Chriſtian confeſſion, it followeth next to ſpeake of prayer and of thankeſgeuing which is nerely con-ioyned to it : for theſe are in order knitte and fittly hanging together with the reſt.

Sch. They be in dede moſt nerely ioyned, for they belong to the firſt table of Gods lawe, and do conteine the principall duties of godlineſſe to-ward God.

Ma. In declaring of prayer, what order ſhall we followe?

Sch. Thys order, maſter, if it ſo pleaſe you : fyrſt to ſhewe who is to be prayed vnto : ſecondly, with what affiance : thirdly, with what affecti-on of hart: and fourthly, what is to be prayed for.

Ma. Firſt then tell me who thou thinkeſt is to be called vpon.

Sch. Surely none but God alone.

Ma. Why ſo?

Sch. Becauſe * our life and ſaluation ſtandeth in the hand of God alone, in whoſe power are all thynges. Sithe then God doth geue vs all that is good, and that a Chriſtian man ought to wiſh and deſire : and ſithe he alone is able in euery * danger to geue helpe and ſuccour and to driue away all perils : it is mete that of hym we aſke all thynges, and in all diſtreſſes flee to
　　　　　　　　　　　　　　P.j.　　　him

hym alone and craue hys helpe . For thys he
him selfe in * hys worde asketh and requireth
as the peculiar and proper worshipping of hys
maiestie.

Ma. Shall we not then do well to call vpon holy
men that are departed out of thys life , or vpon
Angels?

Sch. No . For that were to geue to them an
infinitenesse to be present euery where, or to geue
them being absent an vnderstandyng of our secrete meaninges, that is, as much as à certaine
Godhead , and therewithall partly to conuey
to them our confidence and trust * that ought
to be set wholly in God alone, and so to slide into
idolatrie . But forasmuch as God calleth vs to
hym selfe alone, and doth also with adding an
othe , promise that * he will both heare and helpe
vs , to flee to the helpe of other were an euident token of distrust and infidelitie . And as
touchyng the holy men that are departed out
of thys life , what maner of thyng J pray you
were thys , forsaking the * lyuing God , that
* heareth our prayers , that is most mightye,
* most ready to helpe vs , that * calleth vs vnto hym, that in the worde of truthe promiseth
* and sweareth that with hys diuine power
and succour he will defend vs , forsaking hym,
J say, to flee to men dead, deaffe, and weake,
which neither haue promised helpe nor are able
to relieue vs , to whom God neuer gaue the
office to helpe vs , to whom we are by no Scriptures directed whereupon our * fayth may surely rest , but are vnaduisedly caryed away tru-

sting

sting onely vpon the dreames or rather dotages
of our owne head.

Ma. But God doth to our saluation vse the seruice
of Angels, that wayte vpon vs, and therefore do
heare vs.

Sch. *That is true. But yet it appereth no where
in the word of God, that God would haue vs
pray to Angels, or to godly men decessed. And
sithe fayth resteth vpon *the word of God, and
what is not of fayth *is sinne, I sayd rightly
that it is a sure token of infidelitie to forsake
God, *to whom alone the scriptures do send vs,
and to pray to and craue helpe of Angels, or godly men departed this life, for calling vpon whom
there is not one word in the holy scriptures.

Ma. But seing charitie neuer *falleth out of the
hartes of the godly, euen while they be in heauen
they are carefull for vs and do desire our saluation.

Sch. That can not be denyed, yet it doth not
follow that we must therefore call vpon them,
vnlesse we thinke that we must call for the
helpe and succour of our frendes be they neuer
so farre from vs, onely bicause they beare vs
good will.

Ma. But we oft craue helpe of men that be aliue,
and with whome we are presently conuersant.

Sch. I graunt. For men as they haue *mutually neede one of an others helpe, so hath God
graunted them power one mutually to helpe an
other, yea and he hath expresly commaunded
euery man *to releue his neighbour with such
helpe as he can. We do therefore call vpon men
as ministers of Gods goodnesse, accordyng to

　　　　　P.ij.　　　　　　the

the will of God, looking for helpe and succour of them: but yet so, that all our trust be setled in God alone, and that we recken receiued from him as the springhed of all liberalitie, whatsoeuer is deliuered vs * by the handes of men. Therefore thys is well and orderly done, and no impediment to the calling vpon of God alone, so that we confesse that we do not from els where looke for any good thing, nor settle our whole succour in any other.

Ma. Doest thou then say that we must vse prayer and supplication, like as all other duties of godlinesse, according to the prescription of Gods word, or ells we can not please God?

Sch. Yea verely. For all offense in religion is committed by changing the order and maner apointed by God.

Ma. Hetherto then thou hast sayd that God alone is to be called vpon, putting all our trust in him, and that to hym all thinges as to the springhed of all good thinges are to be imputed, now foloweth next to declare with what confidence we wretched mortall men that are so many wayes vnworthy ought to call vpon the immortall God.

Sch. We are in deede euery way most vnworthy. But we thrust not our selues in proudly and arrogantly as if we were worthy, but we come to hym in the name and vpon trust of * Christ our mediatour, by whom the dore being opened to vs, though we be most base silly wretches, made of clay and slyme, oppressed with conscience of our owne sinnes, we shall not be forbidden to enter, nor shall

haue

haue hard acceſſe to the maieſtie of God and
to the obteyning of his fauor.

Ma. We nede not then, for acceſſe to God, ſome
man to be our meane or interpreter, to commend
and declare our ſute vnto him as it were vnto ſome
worldly Prince.

Sch. Nothing leſſe, vnleſſe we will thinke that
God is,* as men be, bound to one place, that he
can not vnderſtand many thinges but by his ſeruantes, that he ſometime ſlepeth, or hath not ley-
ſure to heare. For, as touching our vnworthi-
neſſe, we haue alredy ſaid that our prayers ſtand
in confidence not vpon any thing in vs, but vpon the only worthineſſe of* Chriſt in whoſe name
we pray.

Ma. Doeſt thou then think that God the father is to
be called vpon in the name and vpon truſt of Chriſt
alone?

Sch. Yea forſoth maiſter. For he alone aboue all
other, moſt ſingularly* loueth vs, ſo farre that he
will do all thinges for our ſakes: he alone is with
God his father, at whoſe right hand he ſitteth
* in moſt hye fauour, that he may obteine what
he will of him: he therfore alone is the mediatour
of God and men, the man Ieſus Chriſt: he alone
I ſay, is the mediator of Redemption, and alſo
of inuocation, in whoſe* name alone the holy
ſcriptures do expreſſly bidde vs to goe vnto God
the father, adding alſo promiſes that he by his interceſſion will bring to paſſe that we ſhal obteine
all that we pray for: Otherwiſe* without Chriſt
the care and hart of God abhorreth men.

Ma. But we doe yet with mutuall* prayers one

P.iij.   helpe

helpe an other, so long as we abide in this world.

Sch. That is true. But we do not therefore set other Mediators in place of Christ, but with conioyned hartes and prayers, according to the rule of charitie and the word of God, we do by one *Mediator call vpon our common Father.

Num.1.b.5.
Heb.9.b.15.

Ma. Thou sayest then that to appoint other mediators to God, or patrones for our cause, but Christ alone, is both against the holy scriptures and therefore against faith, and also conteyneth great iniurie to Christ himselfe.

Sch. Yea forsooth, maister.

Ma. Goe on then.

Sch. The summe is this, that we must come to call vpon God the father, resting vpon affiance of the promises made* to vs by Christ, and trusting vpon his intercession, leauing all respect of our owne worthinesse, and framing our prayers as it were out of the mouth * of Christ. Which doing as it is most agreable to the truth of the Scriptures, so is it most farre from the fault of* arrogancie and presumption.

*Rom.1.b.2.5. and 4.
b.21.24.
2.Cor.1.t.t.20.and.3.b.
4.5.
Galat.3.b.22.
Tit.1.a.2.*

*Mat.b.9.10.
Job.14.b.15.b.26. and
17.t.16.21.and 16.t.23.
24.26.*

*Joh.29.a.1.&
Act.3.c.12.14.*

Ma. Thinkest thou that they which so pray to God as thou sayest ought to haue a good hope to obteine what they aske?

Sch. The Lord himselfe doth also command vs to aske with sure * fayth, making therewith a promise and adding an othe, that it shalbe geuen vs whatsoeuer we aske with fayth. And likewise his Apostles do teach that right prayer procedeth from faith. Therefore we must alway lay this most assured foundation of prayer, that resting

*Mat.21.t.22.
Mar.11.b.22.23.24.
Job.16.t.23.
Iac.1.a.6.& 5.b.15.16.*

resting * vpon sure trust of hys fatherly goodnesse, we must determine that God wyll heare
our prayers and petitions, and that we shall obteyne so farre as it is expedient for vs. Therefore they that come rashly * and vnconsideratly
to prayer, and such as pray douting, and vncertaine of their speding, they do without fruite
powre out vaine and bootelesse wordes.

Ma. I see with what confidence thou sayest we must
call vpon God . Now tell me with what affection
of hart we must come vnto him.

Sch. Our hartes must be sore greeued with fee-
ling of our nede and pouertie, and the miseries
that oppresse vs, so farre forth that we must
burne with great desire of deliuerance from
that griefe, and of Gods helpe which we pray
for. Being thus disposed in hart it can not be but
that we shall most attentiuely and with * most
feruent affection with all maner of prayers and
petitions craue that we desire.

Ma. I see then it is not enough to pray with tong
and voyce alone.

Sch. To pray, not applying thereto our mynde
* and attentiuenesse, without which our prayers
can neuer be effectuall, is not onely to take
frutelesse labor in vaine. (For how shall God
heare vs, when we heede not * nor heare not
our selues?) and not onely to powre out vayne
and frutelesse, but * also hurtfull wordes with
offending Gods maiestie. So farre of is it, that
such prayers can appease the maiestie of God,
that is displeased with our offence.

Ma. How know we that it is thus?

           P.iiij.   *Sch.*

* Iob.4.c.23.24.
2.Cor.3.d.17.

Sch. Sithe God is à spirit, and (as I may so call him) à most pure mynde: he both in all other thinges, and specially in prayer, wherby men as it were talke and common with God, requireth the soule and mynde. And he also testifieth that he will be nere to them onely that

* Psal.145.c.18.19.

call vpon him * truely, that is, with their hart and that their prayers please hym. On the other side God doth worthily abhorre and de-

* Esa.29.c.14.15.
Mat.15.a.8. and 20.c.32.

test their prayers that * fainedly and vnaduisedly vtter with their tong that which they conceiue not with their hart and thought, and deale

* Iere.42.b.10.

* more negligently with immortall God, than they are wont to do with a mortall man. Therefore in prayer the mynde is euer nedefull, but the tong is not alway necessarie.

Ma. But there is some vse of the tong in prayer.

* 1Cal.35.d.28. and 51.c.14.15. and 71.b.21.22.23.
Rom.14.c.11.
Phil.2.d.11.

Sch. Yea forsothe. For meete it is that * the tong do also diligently and earnestly employ all her strength and abilitie to set forth the honor of God, sithe it is aboue all other partes of of the bodie properly created by God to that vse. Moreouer as from a mynde earnestly bent with studie and care, sometime wordes breake out of vs ere we be aware: so oftentimes the very sound of vtterance and the hearing of our owne wordes quickeneth and sharpeneth our mynde, and helpeth the hedefulnesse thereof, and kepeth of and driueth away slacknesse wherewith the hart is continually tempted.

Ma. Sithe it is so, what thinkest thou of them that pray in a strange tong and such as they vnderstand not?

Sch.

Sch. I thinke that they not onely lose their la=
bo₂, but therewith also mocke God him selfe. Fo₂
if LOQVI, to speake, be wittingly to bestow ech
wo₂de in hys right place, they that vtter wo₂des
* which they vnderstand not, chatter rather than
speake, so farre be they from p₂aying . Fo₂ they
play the Parottes rather than men , much lesse
Ch₂istian men . Therefo₂e farre be from godly
men such hypocrisie and mockerie . Fo₂ if Saint
Paule thinke it an absurditie fo₂ a man to speake
to other that speche which they vnderstand not,
bicause wo₂des moue no man but hym that hath
the same language , and affirmeth that both he
that speaketh and he that heareth , shall either
of them be an alien to the other: how much grea=
ter absurditie is it that we our selues be aliens to
our selues , while we vse that speche that we
know not , and goe about to vtter our mea=
ninges and p₂ayers in that tong wherein our
selues are deaffe? Wise men in olde tyme thought
that such men , as most fonde, were most wo₂=
thy to be laughed at.

Ma. I see how hedefull a minde and feruent affection is required in prayer. But tell me, doest thou
thinke this feruentnesse to be naturall and by kinde
planted in our hartes, or that it is a raising vp of our
mindes by God?

Sch. The holy Scriptures do testifie that the
spirit of God raiseth vp vnspeakable *groanings,
whereby our p₂ayers are made effectuall . He
therefo₂e without dout with hys inspiration stir=
reth vp our mindes, and whetteth and helpeth
vs to p₂ay.

             H.j.   *Ma.*

* Cor. 14. 27. &c. ...

Cor. 14. 16

* Cicer. offic.
Tuscu. 5. & de
Oratore.

* Rom. 8. 26.
Ephe. 6. 18.

Ma. How then? when this feruentnesse of minde that can not alway be present, is slacked, or wholly quenched, shall we as it were drousy with slowth, & sleeping, idlely looke for the styrring and mouing of the spirite?

Sch. Nothyng lesse. But rather when we be faynt and slacke in minde, we must * byandby craue the helpe of God, that he will geue vs cherefulnesse and stirre vp our hartes to prayer: For this minde and will we conceaue by the guiding of God.

Ma. Now remayneth that I heare of thee what we ought to aske of God by praier. Is it lawful to aske of God what soeuer commeth in our mind & mouth?

Sch. When men that were strangers to true godlinesse, had such an honest opinion of the maiestie and minde of their Gods, that they thought they ought not to aske of them any thyng vniust or vnhonest: God forbid that we Christians should euer aske any thyng of God in prayer that may * mislyke the minde & will of God. For thys were to do to Gods maiestie most hye iniurie and dishonour, so much lesse may such a prayer please hym or obteine any thyng of hym. And sithe both the wittes of men are * to dull to vnderstand what is expedient for them, and the desires of their hartes are so blinde and wilde, that they not onely neede a guide whom they may followe, but also bridles to restraine them, it were to great an absurditie that we should in prayer be caryed rashly and headlong by our owne affections. By a certayne rule therfore & prescribed forme our prayers ought wholly to be directed.

Ma.

Marginal notes:
* Psal. 51. b. 17.
㉠ vij. 26. b. 40. 41.

Cicero pro domo sua.

* Mat. 7. b. 11.
Joh. 16. c. 23. 24.
Jacob. 4. a. 3.
1. Joh. 5. b. 14.

* Mat. 20. c. 22.
Rom. 8. c. 26. 27.
Jacob. 4. a. 3.

Ma. What rule and forme?

Sch. Euen the same forme of prayer verily,
* which the heauenly scholemaister appointed to
hys disciples, and by them to vs all, wherein he
hath couched in very few pointes all those things
that are lawfull to be askcd of God, and be-
houefull for vs to obteyne: which prayer is after
the author therof called the Lordes prayer. If
therefore we will followe the heauenly teacher
with hys diuine voyce saying before vs, truely
we shall neuer swarue from the right rule of
praying.

Ma. Rehearse me then the Lordes prayer.

Sch. When ye will pray (sayth * the Lorde) say
thus: OVR FATHER WHICH ART IN HEA-
VEN, HALLOWED BE THY NAME. THY KING-
DOME COME. THY WILL BE DONE IN EARTH
AS IT IS IN HEAVEN. GEVE VS THIS DAY
OVR DAILY BREAD. AND FORGEVE VS OVR
TRESPASSES, AS WE FORGEVE THEM THAT
TRESPASSE AGAINST VS . AND LEAD VS
NOT INTO TEMPTATION. BVT DELIVER
VS FROM EVILL. FOR THINE IS THE KING-
DOME, AND THE POWER, AND THE GLORY,
FOR EVER. AMEN.

Ma. Doest thou thinke that we are bound euer so
to render these very wordes, that it is not lawfull in
one worde to varie from them?

Sch. It is no dout that we may vse * other
wordes in praying, so that we swarue not from
the meaning of thys prayer. For in it the Lorde
hath sett out certaine speciall and principall
pointes, to the which vnlesse all our prayers be

M.ij.　　　referred

referred they can not please God. Yet let euery
man aske of God as the present * tyme and hys
neede shall require : and let hym tarry vppon
which part of thys prayer he will, and so long as
he liste, and dilate it in sundry sortes as he will:
for there is no impediment to the contrary, so
that he pray to God with such affiance and affection as I haue before spoken of, and to the
same meanyng that is sett out in thys prayer.

Ma. How many partes hath the Lordes prayer?

Sch. It conteyneth in deede sire petitions, but
in the whole summe there are but two partes.
Whereof the first belongeth onely to the glory of
God, and conteyneth the three former petitions:
the second which conteineth the three later petitions belongeth properly to our commoditie.

Ma. Doest thou so seuer and diuide our profit from
Gods glorie, that thou also makest egall partition
betwene them ?

Sch. I do not seuer thinges conioyned, but for
plainnesse of the whole declaration, I distin-
guishe thynges to be seuerally discerned, for vnderstanding whereunto eche thyng belongeth.
Otherwyse, those thynges that do properly belong to the glorie of God, do also bring most
great profites to vs : and likewise those thynges
that serue our profite, are all referred to the glory of God . * For thys ought to be the end wherunto all thynges must be applyed, thys ought to
be our marke, that Gods glory be most amply
enlarged . Yet in the meane tyme I thinke that
this diuision in partes shall not be inconuenient,
and is made not without reason, but according
to

* Mat. 10.7.&c. and Lu. 12.6.15.b.23.g&c.

The diuision.

The end of all thinges Gods glorie.
* 1.Cor.10.30.31. Col.3.t.s.17.

to the propertie of the thynges them selues, bicause while we aske those thynges that belong properly to the aduauncing of Gods glory, we must for that tyme omitte our owne profites, when yet in the later petitions we may well intend our owne commodities.

Ma. Now let vs somewhat diligently examine the weight of euery worde. Why doest thou call God, FATHER?

Sch. There is great pitth in the vse of this one name FATHER. For it conteyneth two thinges which we haue before sayd to be specially necessarie in praying.

Ma. What be those?

Sch. First I speake, not as to one absent * or deaffe, but I call vpon and pray to God as to one that is present and heareth me, being surely persuaded, that he heareth me when I pray, for els in vaine should I craue hys helpe. And thys surely without all douting I can not so affirme of * any Angell or any man decessed. Secondly we haue before sayd, that sure trust of obteyning is the foundation of right praying. And here is the name of Father and of fatherly loue, and most full of good hope and confidence. It was Gods will therefore to be called by the * sweetest name in earth, by that meane alluring vs to him selfe, that we should without feare come to hym, taking away all douting of hys fatherly hart and good will. For when we determine that he is our father, then being * encouraged with hys spirite, we goe to hym as children vse to goe to their father. God therefore in thys place liked better to

D.iij. be

* Jo.Cal.13.b.13.14.and 36.c.15.17.and.94.b.9 10.11.g 133.a.1.2.g.b.

* Ef.c.63.c.16.

* J.Cal.107.c.17. Rom.15.c.12.

* Rom.8.c.17. Gal.4.a.6.

be called FATHER by name of dere affection *and loue, rather than KING O₂ LORD by termes of dignitie and maiestie, and so therewithall to leaue to vs as to hys * childꝛen, a most rich inheritance of hys fatherly name.

Ma. Shall we then come to God with such sure trust of obteyning as children vse to come to their parentes?

Sch. That farre moꝛe sure ꝗ stedfast is the trust of the good will of God than of men, * Chꝛist the naturall sonne of God best acquainted with hys fathers minde doth assure vs, saying : * Jf ye (sayth he) being euill suffer not your childꝛen to craue in baine, but graunt their requestes, how much moꝛe shall your heauenly father, who is selfe goodnesse ꝗ liberalitie, be bountifull to you! But * Chꝛist, as is afoꝛesayd, bꝛingeth vs all this confidence. Foꝛ God doth not adopt vs oꝛ acknowledge vs to be hys childꝛen, who by nature are the childꝛen of wꝛath, but by Chꝛist.

Ma. What els doth the name of Father teach vs?
Sch. That we come to pꝛayer with that loue, *reuerence, and obedience, which is due to the heauenly father from hys childꝛen, and that we haue such minde as becommeth the childꝛen of God.

Ma. Why doest thou call God OVR FATHER in common, rather than seuerally thine owne father?
Sch. Euery godly man may, J graunt, lawfully call God * hys owne, but such ought to be the communitie and fellowship of Chꝛistian men together, and such dere loue and good will ought euery one to beare to all, that no one of them,

* Mal.1.b.6.

* Joh.1.b.12.
Rom.8.c.15.17.
Gal.4.a.6.7.

* Mat.11.b.27.
Joh.1.c.18.g 10.d.15.

* Mat.7.b.11.
Luc.11.d.13.

* Rom.5.a.1.2.
Gal.4.a.4.5.6.
Eph.2.a.4.5.
1 Joh.1.a.1.

* Malac.1.b.6.
Mat.26.b.39.42.

* Wisd.11.d.24.26.
Rom.1.a.6.
1 Cor.1.a.4.

them, neglecting the rest, care for hym selfe alone,
but haue regard to the publike profite of all. And
therefore in all thys prayer nothyng is priuately
asked, but all the petitions are made in the common name of all . Moreouer, when they that be
of smallest wealth and basest state do call vppon
their common * heauenly father as well as the   *Mal.1.b.10.*
wealthy and such as haue atteyned degrees of   *Iob.2.c.41.*
     1.Cor.1.c.6.
hyest dignitie , we are taught not to disdaine   *Eph.4.a.5.6.*
them to be our brethren that are accepted with
God to the honour of hys childzen. On the other
side, * the most despised and they that in thys   *Deu.10.d.17.18.*
world are vilest , may yet in the meane tyme ease   *Psal.10.b.18. g 68.a.*
     5.6.and 146.b.6.7.8a.
and relieue them selues with thys comfort that
in heauen they haue all one most mighty and
most louing father . Furthermore we that * trust   *Psal.11.b.5.6.7.and*
in God, do rightly professe hym to be our father.   *33.a.1.2. g2.and.37.e.*
     21.16.gk.
For the wicked and vnbeleuing, howsoeuer they   *Rom.1.a.16.and.8.b.*
drede Gods power and iustice, yet can they not   *c9.8.*
haue trust in hys fatherly goodnesse toward thē.
Ma. Why doest thou say that God is in heauen?
Sch. As heauen with round & endlesse circuite
conteyneth all thynges, compasseth the earth,
hemmeth in the seas, neither is there any thyng
or place that is not enuironed and enclosed with
the roomthinesse of heauen, & it is on euery side
wide and open, & alway so present to all thinges,
that all thinges vniuersally are placed as it were
in sight thereof : so we thereby vnderstand that
God possessing * the tower of heauen, therewith   *Psal.11.b.4.c.and*
also holdeth the gouernance of all thynges, is ech   *20.b.6. g 33.b.17. and*
     113.a.4.5.6.6.115.c.3.
where present, seeth, heareth, & ruleth all thyngs.
Ma. Goe forward.

　　　　　　　　　Q.iiij.　　　　　　Sch.

Sch. God is also therefore sayd to be in heauen, bicause that same hyest and * heauenly region doth most royally shine and is garnished with hys diuine and excellent workes. Moreouer by * God reigning in heauen, is declared that he is in eternall and hyest felicitie, while we as yet in earth expulsed from our countrey, like children disherited from their fathers goods, liue miserably & wretchedly in banishment. It is as much therefore to say that * God is in heauen, as if I should call hym heauenly and altogether diuine, that is to say, incomprehensible, most hye, most mighty, most blessed, most good, most great.

Ma. What profite takest thou of these thinges?

Sch. These thynges do pull out of our hartes base and corrupt opinions concerning God, and do instruct our mindes to conceaue à farre other thinking of our heauenly * father, than we vse to haue of earthly parentes, to vse most great reuerence toward hys holy maiestie, and in worshipping maner to looke vp to it and haue it in admiration, and certainly to beleue that he doth harken to and * heare our prayers and desires, to put our whole trust in him that is both gouernor and keper of heauen & earth. And therewith also we are by these wordes admonished not to aske any thyng vnmeete for God, but as speakyng to our heauenly father, to haue our hartes * raised from earth, hye and looking vpward, despising earthly thynges, thinking vpon thinges aboue and heauenly, and continually to aspire to that most blessed felicitie of our father, and to heauen as our * inheritance by our father.

Ma. Thys then so happy a beginning and entrie of prayer being now opened vnto vs, goe to, rehearse me the first Petition.

Sch. First we pray that GODS NAME BE HAL-
LOWED.

Ma. What meaneth that?

Sch. Nothing els but that his glorie be *euery where magnified.

Ma. Why do we aske this first?

Sch. Bicause it is most mete that the children should principally desire and wish the glorie of their father, the *seruantes of their maister, and the creatures of the creator, to be encreased.

Ma. Can Gods glorie be any thing encreased or decreased?

Sch. The glorie of God, forasmuch as it is continually* most ample, can not in dede in it selfe be made either greater by encreasse or lesser by decreasse. For it is not changed with any ad-dition or diminishing as our earthly thinges be. But our prayer is that the name of God be made renomed & knowen to mortall men, & his praise and glory be celebrated here in earth as it is mete to be. And as the infinite power, wisdome, righ-teousnesse, and goodnesse of God, and all his di-uine workes do truely set forth the glorie & maie-stie of God, so we wish that they may appeare noble and glorious* to vs, that the magnificence of the author of them, as it is in it self most large, so it may also in all sortes shine honorable and ex-cellent among vs, and be both priuately and pub-likely praysed and honored.

Ma. Go forward.

R.j.   Sch.

• Eſa.52.b.5.6.
Eʒe.36.b.20.
Rom.2.b.24.

Sch. Moreouer we pray that the holy name of God be not *euill spoken of for our faultes, and as it were diſhonored thereby, but rather that his glorie be by our godlineſſe toward God, and goodneſſe towardes men euery where magnifi-ed. Finally we wiſh that the names of all other

• Joſ.24.c.14.d.23.
pſal.96.a.4.and 97.
b.7.9.and 115.a.3.4.
5c. and 135.6.15.
Rom.1.c.23.
u.Joh.5.d.31.

that in heauen, earth, sea, or els where haue at-tained the names and honors *of Gods and be worſhipped in temples in ſondry formes & with ſondry ceremonies, or to whom men filled with error & falſe fond opinions haue dedicated their hartes as it were chirches, the names (I ſay) of all thoſe imagined and fayned Gods, once vtter-ly deſtroyed, and drowned and defaced with e-ternall forgetfulneſſe, the onely diuine name and maieſtie of God the heauenly father be great and glorious, and that all men in all contreyes may acknowledge it, honorably and holily worſhip and reuerence it, and with pure deſires & hartes pray to it, call vpon it, and craue helpe of it.

Ma. Thou haſt ſaid well. I pray thee goe forward.

Sch. Secondly we pray that GODS KING-

• Mat.4.b.23.and 9.
d.11.
Mar.1.b.14.
Joh.5.b.31.32.

DOME COME, that is, that he ſuffer not the di-uine *truth of his word, which alſo Chriſt calleth the Goſpell of the kingdome, to lie hidden in darkneſſe, but that he dayly more and more bring it abrode, and with his ſuccour mainteine and defend it againſt the deuiſes, craft, and policie of

• 1Mat.13.c.25.e.38.39.
and 17.a.2.3.6.
Luc.16.b.8.
Joh.3.d.19.20.

Satan *and of wicked men, and againſt their fayned treaſons that labor to darken the truth, and to defame it or ſpot it with lyes, and againſt

• Luc.10.a.3. and 20.
a.12. 5c.b.17 18.
Joh.16.a.2.3.and 17.
b.14.15.

the violence *and crueltie of tyrantes, that tra-uaile by all meanes to extinguiſh and oppreſſe
the

the truth & vtterly to roote it vp: so as it may be
made manifest and well knowen to all men that
there is nothing able to resist the inuincible
strength of Gods truth.

Ma. Say on more of the kingdome of God.

Sch. We pray him to bring very many out of
darknesse into the light, instructed with the doctrine of *this holy word, and led by truth, and
that wynning them to his number and holy
companie, that is to say, his Chirch, in the which
he reigneth specially, he will continually gouerne
them *with his spirit, and strengthen them with
his ayde as his soldiars alway earnestly figh-
ting* with their enemies, the band of sinne and
the armye of Satan, that hauing strength and
stedfastnes by his diuine power, restrayning corrupt *and crooked affections, subduing and ta-
ming lustes, conquering, vanquishing, putting
to flight, and chacing away all vices, they may
encrease and enlarge the heauenly common
weale and kingdome, God in the meane tyme
reigning and ruling emperially in their hartes
*by his spirit.

Ma. This we see dayly done.

Sch. These thinges are in deede dayly done, so
as we sufficiently perceiue that* God hath an
eye both to the godly and the wicked, and so as
the kingdome of God may seme to be faire begonne in this world: yet we pray that with continuall encreasing it may grow so farre, that all
the reprobate* that by the motion of Satan
stubburnly and obstinately resist & striue against
Gods truth, and defiling themselues with all

vices and haynous sinnes refuse to submit themselues to the kingdome and dominion of God,
being once subdued and destroyed, and the tyrannie of *Satan himselfe, vtterly rooted out,
and all the enemies slayne, oppressed, and troden
downe, so as nothing may once breath against
the becke and power of God, he alone may euery where gloriously reigne, emperially rule, and
triumph. And as, while God reigneth *by hys
spirit in vs, men haue a certaine communitie
with God in this world, so we pray and wish
that he will also by Christ communicate with vs
in heauen the ioye of the most blessed *kingdome, and the glorie that in euerlasting ages of
worldes shall neuer be changed, that we may
be not onely children *but also heires of our heauenly father. Which desire also we verily nothing
mistrust or doute, that our heauenly father will
one day graunt vs to enioy.

Ma. What foloweth next?

Sch. That GODS WILL BE DONE. For it is
the dutie * of children to frame their life according to the will of their fathers, and not contra-
riwise the parentes to conforme themselues to
the will of their children.

Ma. Doest thou then thinke that men are able to
do any thing against the will of God?

Sch. Surely it is euident and plainly knowen
among all, that many sinnes and foule deedes
are dayly done & committed by mortall men to
the greuous *offending of his will, yet so as God
can not by any force or necessitie be compelled
but that he can most easily bring to effect what
soeuer

foeuer he hath * purpofed to do . We do therefore
pray not only that that may come to paſſe which
he hath decreed, which muſt nedes come to paſſe
bicauſe the will of God doth euer carrie with it à
neceſſitie of performing , but foraſmuch as our
myndes * burning with luſtes , are commonly
caried to deſire and to do theſe thinges that moſt
diſpleaſe God, we pray that he will with the
* mouing of his holy ſpirit ſo change and faſhion
all the willes of vs all to the meanyng and will
of his maieſtie , that we may will or wiſh nothing, much leſſe do any thing, that his diuine
will miſlyketh, and that whatſoeuer we perceiue
* to betyde by his will, we may receiue and ſuffer it, not onely with contented but alſo with
gladſome hartes.

Ma. Whereto doeſt thou adde , that Gods will be
done IN EARTH AS IT IS IN HEAVEN?

Sch. Forſoth, that we be in all thinges ſeruiſable and obedient to Gods maieſtie, after the example of * thoſe heauenly ſpirites whom we call
Angels : and as in heauen there is no rebellion,
ſo in earth alſo there be none any where found
that will or dare reſiſt and ſtriue agaynſt the holy will of God . Yea and when we behold the
* Sunne & Mone, and other ſtarres which we
ſee in the heauen, to be caried with continuall
motion and perpetuall ſtyrring , and with their
beames to lighten the earth, by the will of God,
we behold an example of obedience ſet forth for
vs to follow. Moreouer whereas * God hath in
the holy ſcriptures expreſſly declared his will,
which he hath plainely notified by geuing them

the

*1.Cor.3.d.6.b.14.
Heb.4.d.24.*

the name of his testament or last will, they that varie from the meanyng of the Scriptures, surely do manifestly depart from the wyll of God.

Ma. Now I thinke thou hast sufficiently spoken of the first part of the Lordes prayer, which part conteineth these three pointes that belong onely to the glory of God. Now it is good time for vs to goe forward to the second part which properly concerneth thinges profitable for vs & mete for our cómodities.

Sch. The first point of the second part is, GEVE VS THIS DAY OVR DAILY BREAD.

Ma. What doest thou meane by the name of dayly bread?

*Psal.104.a.14.b.27.
Gen.and 105.c.and
144.d.19.17.12.&c.and
Psal.d.14.13.16.&c.*

Sch. Not onely those thynges that minister vs foode and apparell, but also all other thinges vniuersally that are needefull to the mainteyning, and preseruing of our life and leading it in quietnesse without feare.

Ma. Is there any thing els whereof this word bread doth admonish vs?

*Psal.78.d.18.19.20. &
80.10. and 106.d.14.
Mat.6.b.25.
Luc.16.a.19.
1.Tim.5.b.8.9.*

Sch. That we seeke not and gather together curiously deinty thynges for banketting or precious apparell, or sumptuous housholde stuffe, for pleasure, but that we despising delicacies and excesse, and contented with little, be satisfied with temperate and healthfull diet, and wyth meane and necessarie apparell.

Ma. How doest thou call bread thyne, which thou prayest to haue geuen thee of God?

*Psal.115.c.16.
Mat.7.b.7.8.
1.Cor.4.b.7.
Iam.1.c.17.*

Sch. By Gods gift it becommeth oures, when he liberally geueth it vs for our dayly vses, though by right it be not due to vs.

Ma. Is there any other cause why thou callest it thy bread?   *Sch.*

Sch. By this word we are put in minde that we must get our liuing * with our labour or by other lawfull meane, that being therewith contented we do neuer by couetise or fraude secke any thing of other mennes.

Ma. Seing God biddeth vs get our lyuing by our owne labor, why doest thou aske bread of him?

Sch. It is God alone that geueth * frutefulnesse to the ground, that maketh the land plentifull, and to beare frute abundantly, and therefore it is certaine that in baine shall we wast and spend out all the course of our life in toyle of bodie and trauaile of mynde, * vnlesse it please God to prosper our endeuors. It is mete therefore that we dayly craue in prayer thinges necessarie for our foode and life, at the handes of almighty God, which according to the diuine saying of Dauid, as he created all thinges * so doth also feede and preserue them, and that with thankfull hartes we receiue the same, as it were geuen and reached to vs by God, and deliuered by his owne hand into our handes.

Ma. Thinkest thou that rich men also, which haue flowing plentie and store of all thinges, must dayly craue bread of God?

Sch. In baine * shall we heape together and lay vp plentie, yea such as may for many yeares suffice either our bainglory or our dayly expenses, or necessarie vse, vnlesse God of his grace do make the vse of them healthfull to vs for our life. Yea in baine shall we cramme meate * into our stomach, vnlesse Gods power by which we are rather fed and susteined, than by nourishmentes of

R.iiij.

meate,

meate, Do geue both to the meate power to nourish and to the stomach abilitie to digest it. For which cause, euen after supper, we pray to haue the dayly meate which we haue alredy receiued, to be geuen vs of God, that is to say, to be made lifefull and healthfull to vs.

Ma. Why be added these wordes, DAILY, and THIS DAY.

Sch. To pull out of our hartes the stinges of cares* for to morow, that we be not day and night tormented with them in vaine, and that, the vnsatiable couetise ✦ as it were raging hunger of excessiue wealth* being driuen from our myndes, we diligently doing our dutie, should daily craue of our most liberall father that which he is redy dayly to geue.

Ma. Goe forward to the rest.

Sch. Now foloweth the fifth petition wherein we pray our father to FORGEVE VS OVR TRESPASSES.

Ma. What frute shall we get by this forgeuenesse?

Sch. Most large frute. For where God* hath mercy on humble suters, we shalbe in like place and all one fauor with him, as if we were innocent, holy, and vpright in all partes of our life.

Ma. Is this asking of forgeuenesse necessarie for all men?

Sch. Yea, forasmuch as there liueth no mortall man, that doth not oft* slippe in doing his dutie, and that doth not oft and greuously offend God, yea ✦ *as the scripture beareth witnesse against vs, he that offendeth in any one point is holden manifestly gilty of all, and that he who laboreth

to

to purge him selfe of one sinne to God, shall be
conuicted of a thousand hainous offenses. That
we may therefore obteine forgeuenesse of sinnes,
* one onely hope remayneth, one onely refuge for
all men, the goodnesse and mercy of God through
Christ. As for them that * do not confesse that
they haue sinned, nor do craue pardon of their de=
faultes, but * with that Pharisee do glory in their
innocencie and righteousnesse before God, or ra=
ther agaynst God, they exclude them selues from
the fellowship of ꝑ faythfull, to whom this forme
of prayer is appointed for them to follow, & from
the hauen and refuge of safetie. For thys is it that
Christ sayth, that he came into this worlde, * not
to call the righteous, but sinners to repentance.

Ma. Doest thou affirme that God doth freely forgeue our sinnes?

Sch. * Yea altogether. For els it could not seme
forgeuenesse but amendes: but to make sufficient
amendes for one yea the very least fault, we are
not by any power of ours in any wise able. We
can not therefore with our workes, as it were
with a certaine price, redeme both the offense
past and the peace of God, and make recompense
of like for like, but ought with all lowly prayers
to craue of God pardon both of our fault and punishment, which * pardon is not possible to be ob-
teyned but by onely Christ, and most humbly to
beseche him to forgeue vs.

Ma. But this & the condition which is byandby after limited vnto vs, seme scant to agree fitly together.
For we pray that God so forgeue vs as we forgeue
our detters, or them THAT TRESPASSE A-
GAINST VS.

                  S.j.   **Sch.**

° Mat.18.b.32.33.
Luc.6.c.36.37.38.

Sch. Surely God doth offer vs forgeuenesse vp-on a most reasonable condition, which yet is not so to be taken as if in forgeuing men we should so deserue pardon of God, that the same should be as à certaine recompense made to God. For

° Rom.3.d.24.25. and
11.a.6.
Gal.5.a.4.

then should not Gods forgeuenesse °be freely ge-uen, neither had Christ alone, as the Scriptures teach vs, and as we haue before declared, vpon the crosse fully payed the paines of our sinne due to vs. But vnlesse other do finde vs ready to

° Math.5.a.7.
Luc.6.c.36.
Iacob.2.b.13.

forgeue them, and vnlesse we °in following the mercifulnesse and lenitie of God our father, do shewe our selues to be hys children, he plainly warneth vs to loke for nothyng ells at his hand but extreme seueritie of punishment. He hath therefore appointed our easinesse to forgeue, not as à cause to deserue pardon of God, but to be à pledge to confirme our hartes with sure confi-dence of Gods mercy.

Ma. Is there then no place of forgeuenesse with God left for them that shewe them selues to other not entreatable to forgeue and to lay away displea-sures, and such as will not be appeased?

° Mat.6.b.14.15.and
18.c.24.b.22.29.33.34.

Sch. No place at all. Which both is confirmed and manifest by °many other places of the ho-ly Scripture, and namely by that parable in the Gospell, of the seruaunt which owing hys Lord ten thousand talentes, refused at the same time to forgeue hys fellowe seruaunt one hun-dred pens that he had lent hym, he notably

° Mat.7.a.1.2.
Luc.6.c.37.38.
Iacob.2.b.13.

warneth vs. For °according to the same rule of rigour, and the same example, shall iustice with-out mercy be done vpon hym that can not finde in hys hart to shew lenitie and mercy to other.

Ma.

Ma. Thinkest thou that sutes in law about right and wrong are here condemned?

Sch. * A wickefull minde and reuengefull of iniuries the word of God doth surely condemne. Let contenders at lawe therefore looke well to it, with what minde they sue any man. But the * lawes and ordinances of common right, and their lawfull vse, that is to say, such vse as is directed by the rule of iustice and charitie, are not taken away or condemned by the Gospell of Christ. But in thys part of the Lordes prayer, our mindes are bound to followe the rule of Christian lenitie and loue, * that we suffer not our selues to be ouercome of euill, that is to say, to be drawen so farre by other mens offence, as to haue will to render euill for euill, but rather that we ouercomme euill with good, that is, recompense euill deedes with good deedes, and beare and keepe good will toward our foes, yea and our cruell and deadly enemies.

Ma. Now goe forward to the sixth petition.

Sch. Therein we pray that he LEADE VS NOT INTO TENTATION, BVT DELIVER VS FROM EVILL. For as we before do aske forgeuenesse of sinnes past, so now we pray that * we sinne no more. A thousand feares are sett afore vs, * a thousand periles threatened vs, a thousand snares prouided and layed for vs. And we on our part are so * feble by nature, so vnware to foresee them, so weake to resiste them, that with most small force and occasions we are shooued downe and caryed headlong into deceite.

Ma. Goe forward.

S.ij. Sch.

* Mat.10.b.16.17.
Luc.15.b.3.
1.Cor.1.c.13.15.
* Jer.1.b.14.g q.d.16.
1.Jo).2.c.16.

* Gen.3.a.1.&c.
2.Cor.11.a.3.
Apoc.12.a.4.&20.a.2.
* 1.Pet.5.c.2.

* Ephe.6.d.11.12.

* Joh.16.g.33.
1.Joh.4.a.4.&5.b.4.

* Rom.16.b.20.
Ephe.6.b.10.
..Tim.4.b.17.18.

* Rom.8.a.1.4.6.&c
1.Pet.4.a.1.2.

* Psal.91.a.1.&c.to.
to.and 121.8080.

Sch. Sithe therefore we be most sharpely and continually assaulted, both by * crafty and violent men, and by concupiscence * and our owne lust, by the entysementes of the fleshe, this world, and all meanes of corruption, but specially by that suttle, guilefull, and olde wylye * Serpent the deuill, which like à rauening * Lyon seking whom he may deuoure, together with infinite other malicious * spirites armed with à thousand crafty meanes to hurt vs, is euer ready to destroy vs, and thereby as our weakenesse is, we must needes byandby fall downe and be vtterly vndone, we flee to the faythfull protection of our * almighty most louing father, and pray to hym in these distresses and perills not to forsake vs and leaue vs destitute, but * so to arme vs with hys strength that we may be able not onely to resiste and fight agaynst the lustes of our fleshe, the entisementes of thys worlde, and the force and violent assault of Sathan, but also to ouercome and get the ouerhand of them, and that therefore he will withdrawe our hartes * from vices and offenses, that we fall not into them, nor at any time fayle in our dutie, but may euer lye safe and without feare in * the protection and defense of our most good and also most mighty father.

Ma. Then thou meanest by the name of tentation, the craft and violence of the deuill, the snares and deceites of thys world, and the corruptions and entisementes of our fleshe, by which our soules are moued to sinne, and holden fast entangled.

Sch. Yea forsooth maister.

Ma. Sithe then to catch and entangle men as it were

in.

in snares of tentation, is the proprietie * of Sathan, why doest thou pray that God lead thee not into tentation?

Sch. God as he defendeth and preserueth *them that be hys, that they be not snared with the guiles of Sathan, and so fall into vices & foule sinnes, so from the wicked he *holdeth backe and withdraweth hys helpe and succour, wherof they being destitute, blinded with lust, and running headlong, are catched in all sortes of deceitfull trappes, & caried vnto all kinde of wickednesse, and at length with custome of ill doinges, as it were gathering * à thicke tough skinne, their hartes waxe hard, and so they becomming bondmen and yelding them selues to slauerie to the tyrant Sathan, they runne in ruine to their vndoing and euerlasting destruction.

Ma. There remayneth yet a certaine appendant of the Lordes prayer.

Sch. FOR THINE IS THE KINGDOME, AND THE POWER, AND THE GLORY, FOR EVER. AMEN.

Ma. Why wold Christ haue this conclusion added?

Sch. First, to make vs vnderstand that our sure confidence of obteyning all those thinges that we haue before prayed for, standeth in hys goodnesse and power, and * not in any deseruinges of our owne or of others. For by these wordes is declared, that there is nothing that he which ruleth and gouerneth * the world, in whose dominion and power are all thinges, which most nobly shining in most ample & immortall glory, infinitely excelleth aboue all other, either can not or will not geue vs *when we pray for it, so that it be

S.iij. asked

asked rightly and with assured fayth: that now there be no more douting left in our hartes: which is also declared & confirmed by this worde *A M E N, added to the end of the prayer. More-ouer forasmuch as God alone is able at his owne will * to geue whatsoeuer he hath appointed, it most plainly appeareth that of him alone all these thinges both ought to be asked, and may be ob-teyned, and that there is *no perill or euill of ours so great, which he is not able most easily by hys exceding power, wisedome, and goodnesse, to ouercomme and driue from vs, and also to turne it to our safetie.

Ma. Why is there in the later end mention made of the glory of God?

Sch. To teach vs to conclude all our prayers with prayses of God, for that is * the end where-unto all thinges ought to be referred, that issue ought alwayes to be set before the eyes of vs Christians, for all our doinges and our thoughts to reach vnto, that Gods honour be most large-ly amplified and gloriously set out to sight, how-soeuer yet among men in whose hartes Christi-an religion is not settled, there is scarce any one found, that for his enterprises attempted and pe-rills aduentured, desireth *not glory as a reward of hys deedes and vertues, which yet as not true and sound glory, but vaine shewe and boasting, the Lord vehemently and earnestly commaun-deth them that be hys to eschue.

Ma. Then after entreating of prayer, shall we fittly and in good time adde somewhat of the prayses of God and thankesgeuing?

Sch. Surely * most fittly. For not onely in the
last

laſt end of the Lordes prayer Gods glory is men=
tioned, but alſo the very firſt entrie of it begin=
neth with the glory & prayſes of God . For when
we pray that Gods name be hallowed, what
pray we ells, than that of all hys workes hys
glory be ſtabliſhed, that is, that he be iudged in
forgeuing ſinners, * mercifull : in * puniſhing the
wicked, righteous : in performing hys promiſes,
* true : in heaping daily benefites vpon the vn=
worthy, * moſt good & liberall : that whatſoeuer
* of hys workes we ſee or vnderſtand, we be ther=
by ſtirred to aduance hys glory with prayſes. So
was it Gods will to haue hys glory moſt nerely
ioyned with prayer to hym . For meete it is , that
as when we are touched and troubled * with di=
ſtreſſes, we flee as humble petitioners to Gods
helpe and mercy, ſo we vnfaynedly acknowledge
that by hym we obteine deliuerance frō all euills
and greeues, & that he is to vs the onely author
of all good thinges . For of whom we craue par=
don and all good thinges, to hym when he ge=
ueth them, not in hart & ſpeche to render thankes
were ſurely moſt great vnkindneſſe . We ought
therefore continually with mindefull hart and
due honors to yelde deſerued thanke to the euer=
liuing God.

Ma. Goe forward.

Sch. Moreouer, * to prayſe and magnifie Gods
goodneſſe, iuſtice, wiſedome, and power, and to
geue hym thankes in our owne name and in the
name of all mankinde, is parcell of the worſhip=
ping of God, belonging as properly to hys maie=
ſtie as prayer, wherewith if we do not rightly
worſhip hym, ſurely we ſhall not onely be vnwor=

S.iiij.. thy

* 1.Cor.1.c.12.
Job.1.D.44.
Jer.1.c.21.b.24.
1.Pet.4.c.11.
thy of hys * so many and so great benefites as
vnthankfull persons, but also shall be most worthy of eternall punishmentes , as wicked a-
gaynst God.

Ma. Sithe we also receiue benefites of men , shall it
not also be lawfull to geue them thankes ?

* 1.Cor.12.a.6.b.11.
2.Cor.9.c.9.b.12.
4.Pet.4.c.10.11.
Sch. Whatsoeuer benefites men do to vs, we
ought * to accompt them receiued of God , because he alone in deede doth geue vs them by
the ministery of men . For which cause also,
though men ought not be beneficiall and liberall
* Mat.5.c.16.
4.Pet.2.c.12.
of intent to gett thanke, but to set forth * the glory of God , yet to geue thanke to them that
* Psal.18.a.3.
* moued by kindnesse graunt vs any thing be-
neficially and frendly , why should it not be
* Mat.c.g.41.46.47
Lu:6.b.32.33.34.
Act.24.a.2.3.
lawfull , sithe both * equitie requireth it , and
by law of naturall kindnesse we are bound vnto it ? yea and God him selfe by thys meane
binding vs vnto them, willeth vs to acknowledge the same.

Ma. Doest thou then allow a thankfull minde to
men also ?

Sch. Yea. Sithe our thankfulnesse to men , re-
doundeth to God him selfe, bycause from the
spring hed of his diuine liberalitie as it were by
certaine guiding of water courses, God conuey-
* 1.Cor.12.a.6.b.11.
4.Pet.4.c.10.11.
eth * his benefites to vs by the handes of men.
Therefore if we shew not our selues thankfull
to men, we shall be also vnthankfull to God him
* Psal.115.a.1.
Mat.5.c.16.
2.Cor.4.b.15.and 9.c.
9.b.11.12.13.
1.Pet.2.c.12.
selfe . Only this let vs looke well to , that * his
full glory returne and redound to God alone
as to the author and fountayne of all good
thinges.

Ma. Is there any rule and prescribed forme, for vs
certainly

certainly to followe when we glorifie and honour
God, or geue hym thankes?

Sch. Innumerable prayſes of God, are com=
monly to be ſene ſet out in hys * word, from the
rule whereof if we vary not, we ſhall alway
haue a good paterne to follow in geuing to God
hys glory and honor & in yelding him thankes.
Finally in a ſumme, ſeing the holy ſcriptures do
teach that God is * not only our Lord, but alſo
our Father and Sauiour, and we likewiſe are
hys children and ſeruauntes, it is moſt meete
that we employ all * our life to the ſetting out of
hys glory, render to him his due honor, worſhip,
pray to, and reuerence him, and with hart and
mouth continually thanke hym, ſithe we are to
this * end created by him & placed in this world,
that his immortall glory ſhould be in moſt great
honor among men, and riſe to moſt hye mag=
nificence.

* Maximè in
libro.pſalm.

• Deu.10.d.17.20.and
25.ſ.58.
Mal.1.a.6.7.& 2.b.10.

*Pſal.29.a.1.2.and
34.a.1.2.and 92.a.1.
and 107.tota.
Rom.15.b.6.

*Pro.16.a.4.
Eſa.43.b.7.
Rom.11.c.36.
Coloſ.1.c.16.

¶ *The fourth part.*   *Of Sacramentes.*

Ma. Now hauing ended our treating of the law of
God, of the Crede or Chriſtian confeſſion, and alſo
of prayer and of thankeſgeuing, it reſteth laſt of all
to ſpeake of the Sacramentes and diuine miſteries,
which alway haue prayer and thankeſgeuing ioy=
ned vnto them. Teil me therefore, what is a Sa=
crament?

Sch. * It is an outward teſtifying of Gods
good will & bountifulneſſe toward vs through
Chriſt, by à viſible ſigne repreſenting an inuiſible
and ſpirituall grace, by which the promiſes of

*Mat.3.c.11.and 26.
b.26.and 28.b.19.
Ioh.3.a.5.
Act.2.ſ.38.
Rom.6.a.3.4.
1.Cor.10.b.16.and 11.
c.24.&c.
Gal.3.b.27.
1.Pet.3.b.21.

T.j.   God

God touching forgeuenesse of sinnes and eter=
nall saluation geuen through Christ are as it
were, sealed and the truth of them is more cer=
tainely confirmed in our hartes.

Ma. Of how many partes consisteth a Sacrament?

Sch. Of two partes,* the outward element, or
visible signe, and inuisible grace.

Ma. Why would God so haue vs to vse outward
signes?

Sch. Surely we are not endued with mynde
and vnderstandyng so heauenly and diuine, that
the graces of God do appeare clearely of them
selues to vs as it were to Angels, by this meane
therfore God hath prouided for our weakenesse
that we which are earthly and blinde should in
outward elementes and figures, as it were in
certaine glasses, behold the heauenly graces
which otherwise we were not able to see. And
greatly for our behofe it is that Gods promises
should be also presented to our senses, that they
may be confirmed to our myndes without dou=
tyng.

Ma. But is it not a manifest proofe of infidelitie in
vs, not to geue sure faith to Gods promises, vnlesse
we be vnderpropped with such helpes?

Sch. Surely we are indued* with selender and
vnperfect fayth so long as we are in this world,
and yet we cesse not to be faythfull. For the rem=
nantes of distrust, which alway sticke in our
flesh, do shew the weakenesse of our fayth,* but
yet do not vtterly quench it. These remnantes of
distrust though we can not altogether shake of,
yet we must with continuall encreasing euen to
the

the end of our lyfe trauaile toward *perfection of fayth , in which endeuour the vfe of Sacramentes doth much further vs.

Ma. Is there any other caufe , why the Lord would alfo haue the vfe of externall fignes practifed?

Sch. The Lord dyd furthermore ordeine his myfteries to this end , that they fhould be certaine markes and tokens * of our profeffion: wherby we fhould as it were beare witneffe of our fayth before men , and fhould plainely fhew that we are partakers of Gods benefites with the reft of the godly and that we haue all one concord and confent of Religion with them, and fhould openly teftifie that we are not afhamed * of the name of Chriftians and to be called the Difciples of Chrift.

Ma. What thinkeft thou then of them that thinke they may fpare the diuine myfteries as thinges not of fo great neceffitie?

Sch. Firft they can not fayle this fo godly & due a dutie without * moft haynous offence agaynft God the father, and our Sauiour Jefus Chrift, and alfo agaynft his Church . For what were that els, than indirectly to denye Chrift? And he that vouchfaueth not *to profeffe him felfe a Chriftian, is not worthy to be compted in the number of Chriftians. Agayne they that would refufe the vfe of Sacramentes, as if * they had no nede of them, I thinke were worthy to be condemned not onely of moft hye prefumption, but alfo of vnkinde wickedneffe agaynft God , for afmuch as they do defpife not onely the helpes of their owne weakeneffe , but alfo God him felfe the au-

T.ij. thor

° 1.Cor.6.a.1.
1.Theſ.5.c.19.

thoꝛ of them, refuſe* his grace, and (as much as
in them lyeth)extinguiſh his ſpirit.

Ma. Thou conceiueſt well the right vnderſtanding
concerning the viſible ſignes and outward vſe of the
Sacramentes. But whereas ſecondly thou geueſt to
the Sacramentes the ſtrength & efficacie to ſeale and
confirme Gods promiſes in our harts, thou ſemeſt to
aſſigne to them the proper offices of the holy ghoſt.
Sch. To lighten and geue bꝛight clereneſſe to

* Luc.12.b.12.
Joh.1.b.33.and 6.g.
63.and 14.b.17.b.26.
1.Cor.12.a.a.6.gc.

mens* myndes and ſoules, and to make their
conſciences quiet and in ſecuritie, as they be in
deede, ſo ought they to be accompted the pꝛopꝛe
woꝛke of the holy ghoſt alone, and to be imputed
to him, and this pꝛayſe not to be tranſferred to
any other. But this is no impediment but that
God may geue to his myſteries the ſecond place
in quieting and ſtabliſhing our myndes and con=
ſciences, but yet ſo that nothing be abated from
the vertue of his ſpirit. Wherfoꝛe we muſt deter=
mine, that the outward element hath neither

* Job.1.b.33.
Act.1.a.5.g 10.g.47.

*of it ſelfe, noꝛ in it ſelfe incloſed the foꝛce and
efficacie of the Sacrament, but that the
ſame wholly floweth from the ſpirit of God, as
out of a ſpꝛinghed, and is by the diuine myſte=
ries, which are oꝛdeined by the Loꝛd foꝛ this
end, conueyed vnto vs.

Ma. How many Sacramentes hath God ordeined
in his Chirch?
Sch. Two.
Ma. Which be they?

* Mar.28.c.16.ag.9 28.
b 29.
Joh.3.a.5.and 6.f.51.
Tit.3.b.5.

Sch. *Baptiſme, and the holy Supper, which
are commonly vſed among all the faythfull. Foꝛ
by the one we are boꝛne agayne, and by the other
we

we are nouriſhed to euerlaſtyng lyfe.

Ma. Then tell me firſt what thou thinkeſt of Baptiſme.

The deſcriptiõ of Baptiſme.

Sch. Whereas by nature we are * the children of wrath, that is, ſtraungers from the Chirch, which is Gods houſehold, baptiſme is as it were * a certaine entrie by which we are receiued into the Chirch, wherof we alſo receiue a moſt ſubſtantiall teſtimonie, that we are now * in the number of the houſehold, & alſo of the children of God, yea and that we are ioyned and graffed into * the bodie of Chriſt, and become his members and do grow into one bodie with hym.

* Ephe.2.2.3.

* Math.28.19. Mar.16.b.16. Joh.3.a.5. Tit.3.b.5.

* Rom.2.b.17.18.19. Ephe.2.b.19.

* 1.Cor.6.c.15.and 12.b.12. Gal.3.b.27. Eph.4.d.15.16.and 5.g.30.

Ma. Thou ſaydeſt before that a Sacrament conſiſteth of two partes, the outward ſigne, and inward grace. What is the outward ſigne in Baptiſme?

Sch. * Water, wherein the perſon Baptiſed is dipped, or ſprincled with it, IN THE NAME OF THE FATHER, AND OF THE SONNE, AND OF THE HOLY GHOST.

* Mat.3.b.16.and 28. h.19. Joh.3.a.5.c.23. Act.2.g.38.

Ma. What is the ſecret and ſpirituall grace?

Sch. It is of two ſortes, that is, * forgeueneſſe of ſinnes and regeneration, both which in the ſame outward ſigne haue their full and expreſſe reſemblance.

* Mar.1.a.4. Joh.3.a.5. Act.2.c.38. Tit.3.b.5.

Ma. How ſo?

Sch. Firſt, as the vncleanneſſes of the bodie are waſhed away with water, ſo the * ſpottes of the ſoule are waſhed away by forgeueneſſe of ſinnes. Secondly * the begynnyng of regeneration, that is, the mortifying of our nature is expreſſed by dipping in the water, or by ſprinklyng of it. Finally when we byandby riſe vp agayne out of

* Act.22.d.16. Eph.5.d.26. Tit.3.b.5.6.

* Joh.3.a.5. Rom.6.a.3.4.b.6.7. &c. Tit.3.b.5.

C.iij.　　the

the water vnder which we be for a short tyme, the new lyfe which is the other part and the end of our regeneration is therby represented.

Ma. Thou semest to make the water but a certaine figure of diuine thynges.

* Joh.3.a.5;
Act.22.c.10.
Ephe.5.b.26.
Tit.3.b.5.

Sch. * It is a figure in dede, but not empty or deceitefull, but such as hath the truth of the thyngs them selues ioyned and knit vnto it . For as in Baptisme God truly deliuereth vs forgeuenesse of sinnes and newnesse of lyfe, so do we certainely receiue them .

* Joh.14.a.6.b.17.
Rom.3.a.4.
Heb.10.b.23.

* For God forbid that we should thinke that God mocketh and deceiueth vs with vayne figures.

Ma. Do we not then obteine forgeuesse of sinnes by the outward washing or sprinkling of water?

* Mat.26.c.28.
Ephe.1.b.7.&.5.b.25.
Col.1.c.14.20.
Tit.3.b.5.6.
Apoc.1.b.5.

Sch. No. For onely Christ hath * with his bloud washed & cleane washed away the spottes of our soules. This honor therefore it is not lawfull to geue to the outward element. But the holy Ghost as it were sprinkling * our consciences with that holy bloud, wipyng away all the spots of sinne, maketh vs cleane before God. Of this clensing of our sinnes we haue a seale and pledge in the Sacrament.

* Joh.3.a.5.
Rom.2.b.15.16.
Heb.9.b.14.and 10.b.
22.

Ma. But whence haue we regeneration?

* Rom.6.a.3.&c.Col.2.

Sch. None other wayes but from the death & resurrection of Christ. * For by the force of Christes death, our old man is after a certaine maner crucified & mortified, and the corruptnesse of our nature is as it were buried, that it no more lyue & be strong in vs. And by the beneficiall meane of his resurrection he geueth vs grace to be newly formed vnto a new lyfe to obey the righteousnesse of God.

Ma.

Ma. Do all generally and without difference receiue this grace?

Sch. *The only faithful receiue this frute, but the
vnbeleuing in refusing the promises offered them
by God, shut vp the entrie agaynst them selues,
& go away empty. Yet do they not therby make
that the Sacramentes lose their force & nature.

Ma. Tell me then briefly in what thinges the vse of
Baptisme consisteth.

Sch. In faith and repentance. For * first we
must with assured confidence hold it determined in our hartes : that we are cleansed by the
bloud of Christ from all filthynesse of sinne, and
so be acceptable to God and that his spirit dwelleth within vs. And then we must continually with all our power and endeuor trauaile in
* mortifieng our flesh and obeyeng the righteousnesse of God, and must by godly lyfe declare to
all men that we haue in Baptisme as it were
* put on Christ, and haue his spirit geuen vs.

Ma. Sith infantes can not by age performe those
things thatthou speakest of, why are they baptised?

Sch. That fayth and repentance go before Baptisme, is required onely in persones so growen
in yeares * that by age they are capable of both.
But to infantes the promise * made to the Chirch
by Christ, in whose faith * they are baptised, shall
for the present tyme be sufficient, and then afterward when they are growen to yeares, they
must nedes them selues acknowledge the truth
of their baptisme, and haue the force therof to be
liuely in their soules and to be represented in
their lyfe and behauiours.

             T.iiij.   *Ma.*

Ma. How shall we know that infantes ought not to be kept from baptisme?

Rom.3.a.3.4.and 4.b.11.
Heb.10.b.23.

Sch. Seyng God * which neuer swarueth from truth, nor in any thyng strayeth from the right way, dyd not exclude infantes * in the Iewish Chirch from Circumcision, neither ought our infantes to be put backe from baptisme.

Gen.17.b.10.11.12. &c.
Luc.1.f.59.g.2.c.21.
Act.7.a.8.
Phil.3.a.5.

Ma. Thinkest thou these so like, and that they both haue one cause and order?

Deu.10.b.16.and 30.b.6.
Iere.4.a.4.

Sch. Altogether. For, as Moses * and all the Prophetes do testifie that Circumcision was a signe of repentance, so doth Saint Paul teach that it was a Sacrament of faith. Yet the * Iewes children beyng not yet by age capable of faith and repentance, were neuerthelesse circumcised, by which visible signe God shewed him selfe in the old testament to be the father of yong children and of the sede of his people. Now sithe it is certaine that the grace of God is both * more plentifully poured and more clerely declared in the Gospell by Christ, then at that tyme it was in the old Testament by Moses, it were a great indignitie if the same grace should now be thought to be either obscurer or in any part abated.

Rom.2.b.23.29.and 4.b.11.
Gen.17.a.7.b.10.11. 12.g.

Act.2.c.17.18.and 10.g.45.
2.Co.3.b.6.7.8.9.g. Gal.3.c.23.24. Ro.3.b.3.6.

Ma. Go on forward.

Mat.18.a.3.4.b.10. and 19.b.14.
Luc.18.b.15.16.17.
Rom.4.c.16.b.23.24.
1.Pet.3.a.2.

Sch. Sith it is certaine that our infantes haue the force and as it were the substance of baptisme common with vs, they should haue wrong done them, if the signe, which is inferior to the truth it selfe, should be denyed them, and the same, which greatly auayleth to testifying of the mercie of God and confirmyng his promises, beyng taken away, Christians should be defrauded

of

of à singular comfort which they that were in old tyme enioyed, and so should our infantes be more hardly dealt with in the new testament vnder Christ, then was dealt with the Iewes infantes in the old testament vnder Moses. Therfore most great reason it is, that by baptisme as by the print of à seale, it be assured to our infantes that they be heyres of Gods grace, and of the saluation promised to the sede of the faythfull.

Ma. Is there any more that thou wilt say of this matter?

Sch. *Sithe the Lord Christ calleth infantes vnto hym, and commaundeth that no man forbid them to come, embraceth them when they come to hym, and testifieth that to them the kingdome of heauen belongeth: whom God vouchsaueth to be in the heauenly palace, it seemeth à great wrong that men should forbid them the first entrie and doore thereof, and after à certaine maner to shutt them out of the Christian common weale.

Ma. It is so. But whereas thou diddest say before that children after they were growen more in yeares ought to acknowledge the truth of their Baptisme, I would thou shouldest now speake somewhat more plainly thereof.

Sch. Parentes and Scholemaisters did in olde time diligently instruct their children as soone as by age they were able to perceaue & vnderstand, in the first principles of Christian Religion, that they might sucke in godlinesse almost together with the nourses milke, and straight waies after their cradle, might be nourished with the tender foode of vertue towardes that blessed life. For

U.j.   the

the which purpose also little short bookes which we name Catechismes, were written: wherein the same, or very like matters, as we now are in hand with, were entreated vpon. And after that the children seemed to be sufficiently trained in the principles of our Religion, they brought and offered them vnto the Byshop.

Ma. For what purpose did they so ?

Sch. That children might after Baptisme do the same which such as were elder who were also called *Catechumini*, that is, scholers of Religion, did in olde time before, or rather at Baptisme it selfe. For the Bishop did require and the children did render reason and accompt of their Religion and fayth: and such children as the Bishop iudged to haue sufficiently profited in the vnderstanding of Religion he allowed, and laying hys handes vpon them and blessing them let them depart. This allowance and blessing of the Bishop our men do call confirmation.

Ma. But there was an other confirmation vsed of late.

Sch. In steede of thys most profitable and ancient confirmation, they conueyed à deuise of their owne, that is, that the Bishop should not examine children whether they were skilled in the preceptes of Religion or no, but that they should anoint young infantes vnhable yet to speake, much lesse to geue any accompt of their fayth, adioyning also other ceremonies vnknowen vnto the holy Scripture and the Primitiue Chirch. This inuention of theirs they would nedes haue to be à sacrament, & accompted it in maner equall in dignitie with Baptisme: yea some of them prefer-

fer-

ferred it also before Baptisme. By all meanes they would that thys their confirmation should be taken for à certaine supplying of Baptisme, that it should thereby be finished and brought to perfection: as though Baptisme els were vnperfect, and as though children who in Baptisme had put vpon them Christ with hys benefites, without their confirmation were but halfe Christians : than which iniurie no greater could be done against the diuine Sacrament, and against God him self, & Christ our Sauior, the author and founder of the holy Sacrament of Baptisme.

Ma. It were to be wished therfore that the ancient maner and vsage of examining children were restored againe.

Sch. Uery much to be wished surely. For so shold parentes be brought to the satisfying of their dutie in the godly bringing vp of their children, which they now for the most part do leaue vndone, and quite reiecte from them : which part of their dutie if Parentes or Scholemaisters, would at thys time take in hand, do, & throughly performe, there would be à marueilous consent and agreement in Religion and fayth, which is now in miserable sort torne asunder : surely all should not either lye so shadowed, and ouerwhelmed with the darkenes of ignorance, or with dissentions of diuers and contrary opinions be so disturbed, dissolued, and dissipated, as it is at this day : the more pitie it is, and most to be sorrowed of all good men for so miserable à case.

Ma. It is very true that thou sayest. Now tell me the order of the Lordes supper.

Sch. It is euen the same which the Lord Christ   The Lordes Supper.

did institute. Who in the same night that he was betrayed, *TOOKE BREAD, AND WHEN HE HAD GEVEN THANKES, HE BRAKE IT, AND GAVE IT TO HIS DISCIPLES, SAYING: TAKE, EATE, THIS IS MY BODY, WHICH IS GEVEN FOR YOV. DO THIS IN REMEMBRANCE OF ME. LIKEWISE, AFTER SVPPER, HE TOOKE THE CVP, AND WHEN HE HAD GEVEN THANKES, HE GAVE IT TO THEM, SAYING: DRINKE YE ALL OF THIS. FOR THIS IS MY BLOVD OF THE NEW TESTAMENT WHICH IS SHED FOR YOV, AND FOR MANY, FOR REMISSION OF SINNES. DO THIS AS OFT AS YE SHALL DRINKE IT IN REMEMBRANCE OF ME. FOR SO OFT AS YE SHALL EATE THYS BREAD, AND DRINKE OF THIS CVP, YE SHALL SHEW THE LORDES DEATH TILL HE COME. This is the forme & order of the Lordes Supper, which we ought to hold and holily to kepe till he come.

Ma. For what vse?

Sch. * To celebrate and reteine continually a thankfull remembrance of the Lordes death, and of that most singular benefit which we haue receiued therby, and that as in Baptisine we were ones borne agayne, so with the Lordes Supper we be alway fed and susteined to spirituall and euerlastyng lyfe.

Ma. Thou sayest then that it is enough to be ones Baptised, as to be ones borne, but thou affirmest that the Lordes Supper, like as foode, must be often vsed.
Sch. Yea forsoth maister.
Ma. Doest thou say that there are two partes in this Sacrament also, as in Baptisine?

Sch.

Sch. Yea. The one part the bred and wine, the outward signes which are seen with our eyes, handled with our handes, and felt with our tast: the other part, Christ hym selfe with whom our soules as with their propre foode are inwardly nourished.

Ma. And doest thou say, that all ought alike to receiue both partes of the Sacrament.

Sch. Yea verily maister. For sith the Lord hath expressly so commaunded, it were a most hye offense in any part to abridge his commandement.

Ma. Why would the Lord haue here two signes to be vsed?

Sch. First he seuerally gaue the signes both of hys body and bloud, that it might be the more playne expresse image of his death, which he suffered his body being torne, his side pearced, and all his bloud shed, and that the memory thereof so printed in our hartes should sticke the deper. And moreouer that the Lord might so prouide for and helpe our weakenesse, and thereby manifestly declare, that as the bred for nourishment of our bodyes, so his body hath most singular force and efficacie spiritually to feede our soules: and as with wyne mennes hartes are cheared, and their strength confirmed, so with hys bloud our soules are releued and refreshed: that certaynely assuring our selues that he is not onely our meate, but also our drinke, we do not any where ells but in him alone, seeke any part of our spirituall nourishment and eternall life.

Ma. Is there then not an onely figure but the truth it selfe of the benefites, that thou hast rehearsed, deliuered in the supper?

U.iij.　　Sch.

Sch: what els ! For sithe Christ is * the truth it selfe, it is no doubt but that the thing which he testifieth in wordes and representeth in signes, he performeth also in deede and de=liuereth it vnto vs, and that he as surely ma= keth them * that beleue in hym, partakers of hys body and bloud , as they surely know that they haue receiued the bred and wyne with their mouth and stomack.

Ma. Sithe we be in the earth, and Christes body in heauen, how can that be that thou sayest?

Sch. we must lift our soules and hartes from earth,* and rayse them vp by fayth to heauen, where Christ is.

Ma. Sayest thou then the meane to receiue the bo-dy and bloud of Christ standeth vpon fayth?

Sch. Yea. For when * we beleue that Christ dyed, to deliuer vs from death , and that he rose agayne to procure vs life, we are parta= kers of the redemption purchaced by hys death, and of hys life and all other hys good things, and with the same conioyning wherewith the hed and * the members are knitt together, he coupleth vs to hym selfe by secret and mar= uellous vertue of hys spirite, euen so that we be members of hys body, and be of hys flesh and bones,and do growe into one body with hym.

Ma. Doest thou then, that this conioyning may be made , imagine the bred and wyne to be changed into the substance of the flesh and bloud of Christ?

Sch. There is no neede to inuent any such change. For both the holy scriptures, and the

best

best and most auncient expositors do teach that by baptisme we are * likewise the members of Christ, and are of hys flesh and bones and do growe into one body with hym, when yet there is no such change made in the water.

Ma. Goe on.

Sch. In both the sacramentes, the substances of the outward thinges not changed, but * the word of God and heauenly grace coming to them, there is such efficacie, that as by baptisme we are once * regenerate in Christ, and are first as it were ioyned and grafted into hys body : so, when we * rightly receiue the Lordes supper, with the very diuine nourishment of hys body and bloud, most full of health and immortalitie, geuen to vs by the worke of the holy ghost, and receiued of vs by fayth as the mouth of our soule, we are continually fedde and susteyned to eternall * life, growing together in them both into one body with Christ.

Ma. Then Christ doth also otherwise than by hys supper only geue hym selfe vnto vs and knitteth vs to hym selfe with most streight conioyning.

Sch. Christ did then principally geue hym selfe to vs to be the author of our saluation, when he gaue * hym selfe to death for vs, that we should not perish with deserued death. By the * Gospell also he geueth hym selfe to the faythfull, and plainely teacheth that he is that liuely bred that came downe from heauen to nourish their soules that beleue in him. And also*in Baptisme, as is before said, Christ gaue him selfe to vs effectually, for that he then made vs Christians.

U.iiij.   *Ma.*

Ma. And sayest thou that there are no lesse straight bandes of conioyning in the supper?

Sch. In the Lordes supper, both that communicating which I spake of, is confirmed vnto vs, * and is also encreased, for that eche man is both by the wordes and mysteries of God ascertained that the same belongeth to him selfe, and that Christ is by a certaine peculiar maner geuen to him, that he may most fully and with most nere coniunction enioy him, in so much that not onely our soules are nourished * with his holy body and bloud as with their proper foode, but also our bodies, for that they partake of the sacramentes of eternall life, haue as it were by a pledge geuen them, à certaine hope assured them of resurrection and immortalitie, that at length Christ * abyding in vs and we agayne abiding in Christ, we also by Christ abyding in vs, may obteine not only euerlasting life, but also the glory which his father gaue him. In a summe I say thus: As I imagine not any grosse ioyning, so I affirme that same secret and maruellous communicating of Christes body in his supper to be most nere, and strait, most assured, most true, and altogether most high and perfect.

Ma. Of this that thou hast sayd of the Lordes supper, mē semes I may gather, that the same was not ordeined to this end, that Christes body should be offred in sacrifice to God the father for sinnes.

Sch. It is not so offred. For he, when he did institute his supper, commaunded vs * to eate his body, not to offer it. As for the prerogatiue * of offering for sinnes, it perteineth to Christ alone, as to hym which is the eternall priest, which also

when

when he dyed vpon the crosse, once made that onely and euerlasting sacrifice for our saluation, and fully performed the same for euer. For vs there is nothing left to do, but to take the vse and benefite of that eternall sacrifice bequethed vs by the Lord hym selfe, which we chiefely do in the Lordes Supper.

Ma. Then I perceaue the holy Supper, sendeth vs to the death of Christ, and to hys sacrifice once done vpon the Crosse, by which alone God is appeased toward vs.

Sch. It is most true. For by bread and wine the signes, is assured vnto vs, * that as the body of Christ was once offred à sacrifice for vs to recon= cile vs to fauour with God, and hys bloud once shed to washe away the spottes of our sinnes, so now also in hys holy Supper * both are geuen to the faithfull, that we surely know that the recon= ciliation of fauor perteineth to vs, and may take and receaue the fruite of the redemption purcha= sed by hys death.

Ma. Are then the onely saythfull fed with Christes body and bloud?

Sch. They onely. For to whom he communica= teth hys body, * to them (as I sayd) he commu= nicateth also euerlasting life.

Ma. Why doest thou not graunt that the body and bloud of Christ are included in the bread and cup, or that the bread and wine are changed into the sub= stance of hys body and bloud?

Sch. Because that were to bring in dout * the truth of Christes body, to do dishonor to Christ him selfe, and to fill them with abhorring that re= ceaue the Sacrament, if we should imagine hys

X.j.   body

body either to be inclosed in so narrow à roome,
* or to be in many places at once, * or hys flesshe to
be chawed in our mouth with our teeth, and to
be bitten small and eaten as other meate.

Ma. Why then is the communicating of the sacrament damnable to the wicked, if there be no such
chaunge made?

Sch. Because they come to the holy and diuine
mysteries * with hypocrisie and counterfaiting,
and do wickedly profane them, to the great iniurie and dishonor of the Lord him selfe that ordey-
ned them.

Ma. Declare then, what is our dutie, that we may
come rightly to the Lordes Supper.

Sch. Euen the same that we are taught in the
holy Scriptures, namely, * to examine our selues
whether we be true members of Christ.

Ma. By what markes and tokens shall we manifestly
finde it?

Sch. First, if * we hartily repent vs of our sinnes,
which droue Christ * to death, whose mysteries
are now deliuered vs. Next if we stay our selues
& rest * vpon à sure hope of Gods mercy through
Christ, with à thankfull * remembrance of our redemption purchaced by hys death. Moreouer if
we conceaue an earnest minde and determined
purpose to lead our life godlily * hereafter. Finally, if, seing in the Lordes Supper is conteyned also * à tokening of frendship & loue among
men, we beare brotherly loue to * our neighbors,
that is, to all men, without any euill will or
hatred.

Ma. Is any man able fully & perfectly to performe
all these thinges that thou speakest of?

Sch.

Sch. Full perfection in all pointes wherin nothing may be lacking, can not be found * in man
so long as he abideth in thys worlde. Yet ought
not the imperfection that holdeth vs, keepe vs
backe from comming to the Lordes Supper,
which the Lord willed to be à helpe to our imperfection and weaknesse. Yea if we were perfect, there should be no more neede of any vse of
the Lordes Supper among vs. But hereto these
things that I haue spoken of do tend, that euery
man bring with hym to the supper, * repentance,
* fayth, and * charitie, so nere as possibly may be,
syncere and vnfained.

Ma. But when thou sayedst afore that the Sacramentes auaile to confirmation of fayth, how doest
thou now say that we must bring fayth to them?

Sch. These sayinges do not disagree. For there
must be * fayth begonne in vs, to the nourishing
and strengthening wherof the Lorde hath ordeined the Sacramentes, which bring great effectuall helpes to * the confirming and as it were
sealing the promises of God in our hartes.

Ma. There remayneth yet for thee to tell, to
whom the ministration of the Sacramentes properly
belongeth.

Sch. Sithe the duties and offices of feeding the
Lordes flocke with Gods worde, and the mini-
string of * Sacramentes, are most nerely ioyned
together, there is no doute that the ministration therof properly belongeth to them to whom
the office of publike teaching is committed. For
as the Lorde * him selfe at hys supper exercising
the office of the publike minister did set forth hys
owne example to be followed, so dyd he com-

X.ij.   mitte

*Mat. 19.4.21.
Rom. 7. b. 18.
1. Cor. 13. c. 9. 10. 12.
Phil. 3. a. 12. 13.

*Iere. 14. b. 7. and
19. c. 13.
Ioel. 2. d. 12. 13.
* Galat. 1. a. 6.
Col. 1. a. 4. 2. 23. and
2. a. 1.
1. Tim. 1. a. 1.
2. Tim. 1. b. 3.

*Mat. 17. b. 19.
Rom. 11. b. c.
2. Cor. 2. b. 6.

*Rom. 1. b. 17.
1. Thess. 3. c. 10.
2. Thess. 1. a. 3.
Heb. 6. a. 1.

*Act. 7. f. 42.
Rom. 4. b. 11. and 19.
b. 2. and 6. a. 4.
Gal. 3. b. 27.
Ephe. 2. c. 11. 12. and
4. a. 1.
Col. 2. b. 11. 12.
1. Pet. 3. b. 21.

*Mat. 28. b. 19.
Mar. 16. b. 15.
Act. 2. f. 38. 41. and b.
b. 12. d. 35. 36. 37.

*Math. 26.
Mark. 14.
Luke. 22.
1. Cor. 11.

mitte the offices of baptising and teaching pecu=
liarly to hys Apostles.

Ma. Ought the Pastors to receaue all indifferently
without choise, to the Sacramentes?

Sch. In olde tyme when men growen, * and of
full yeares, came to our religion, they were not
admitted so much as to baptisme, vnlesse there
were first assurance had of their fayth in the
chiefe articles of Christian religion. Now be=
cause onely infantes are baptised, there can be no
choise made. Otherwise it is of the Lordes Sup=
per, whereunto sithe none come but they that are
growen in yeares, if any be openly knowen to be
vnworthy, the Pastor ought not to admitte hym
to the Supper, because it can not be done with=
out profane abuse of the Sacrament.

Ma. Why did the Lord then not exclude the * trai-
tor Iudas from communicating of hys Supper?

Sch. Because his wickednesse, howsoeuer it was
knowen to the Lord, was not yet at that tyme
openly knowen.

Ma. May not the ministers then put backe hy-
pocrites?

Sch. No, so long as their wickednesse is secrete.

Ma. Sithe then both good and bad do indifferently
and in common vse the sacramentes, what sure and
stedfast trust of consciences can be in them, which
thou euen now didst affirme?

Sch. Though * the vngodly, so much as concer=
neth them selues, do not receaue the giftes of
God offred in the Sacramentes, but do refuse,
and disappoint them selues, yet * the godly which
by fayth seeke Christ and hys grace in them, are
neuer disappointed or defrauded of a most good
conscience

conscience of minde, and most sweete comfort, by an assured hope of saluation & of perfect felicitie.

Ma. But if any Pastor do either him selfe know, or be priuily informed that they be vnworthy, may he not exclude them from the communion?

Sch. Such he may both in publike sermons admonishe, so he vtter them not by name, or blott them with stayne or infamie, but pinch them and reproue them onely with suspicion of their owne conscience and with coniecture, and he may also priuately greuously threaten them, but put them backe from the Communion he may not, vnlesse the lawfull examination and iudgement of the Chirch be first had.

Ma. What remedie is then to be found and vsed for this mischiefe?

Sch. In Chirches well ordered and well mannered, there was, as I sayd before, ordeined and kept à certaine forme and order of gouernance. There were chosen Elders, that is, ecclesiasticall magistrates, to holde and keepe the discipline of the Chirch. To these belonged, the authoritie, looking to, and correction like Censors.* These, calling to them also the Pastor, if they knew any that either with false opinions, or troublesome errours, or vaine superstitions, or with corrupt and wicked life, brought publikely any great offense to the Chirch of God, and which might not come without profaning the Lordes Supper, did put backe such from the communion and reiected them, & did not admit them againe till they had with publike penance satisfied the Chirch.

Ma. What measure ought there to be of publike penance?

X.iij.　　　Sch.

1.Cor.10.g.32.
Rit.3.c.10.11.
1.Thess.5.c.14.
2.Thess.3.b.14.15.

2.Cor. 2.b. 6. and
7.A.9.10.

Sch. Such as goe about with deuises of false opinions * to hurt true godlinesse and shake religion, or with corrupt and wicked life haue raised greuous & publike offenses, it is meete that they make * publike satisfaction to the Chirch whom they haue so offended, that is, syncerely to acknowledge and confesse their sinne before the whole congregation, and openly to declare that they be hartily sorry that they haue so greuously offended almighty God, and as much as in them lay haue dishonored the Christian religion which they haue professed, and the Chirch wherin they were accompted, & that not by their sinne onely, but also by pernicious example they haue hurt other, and therefore they craue and pray pardon first of God, and then of hys Chirch.

Ma. What shall then be done?

Sch. Then they must humbly require & pray that they may be againe receaued into the Chirch, which, by their deseruing, they were cast out of, and to the holy mysteries therof. In short summe,
* 2.Cor.i. b.6.7.8.10
there must in publike penance be such moderation vsed, that neither by too much seueritie, he that hath sinned do despeire, nor on the other side by too much softnesse, the discipline of the Chirch decay, and the authoritie therof be abated, and other be encouraged & boldened to attempt the
* 1.Cor.2.b.6.:0.
like. But when by the iudgement of the Elders and the Pastor, both the punishment of hym that sinned, and the example of other is satisfied, then he that had ben excommunicate was wont to be receaued againe to the Comunion of the Chirch.

The conclusion with an exhortation.
Ma. I see, my childe, that thou well vnderstandest the summe of Christian godlinesse. Now it resteth

that

that thou so direct thy life by the rule of this godly
knowledge, that thou seeme not to haue learned
these things in vaine. For not they that *onely heare
and vnderstand Gods worde, but they that follow
Gods will and obey hys commaundement, shall be
blessed. Yea that seruant that knoweth hys maisters
will and followeth it not, shall be *more greuously
beaten. So little profiteth the vnderstanding of godlinesse and true religion, vnlesse there be ioyned to it
vprightnesse of life, innocencie, and holinesse. Goe
to therefore, my childe, bend all thy care & thought
hereunto that thou fayle not in thy dutie, or swarue
at any time from thys rule and prescribed forme of
godly life.

Sch. I will do my diligence, worshipful maister,
and omitt nothing, so much as I am able to do,
and with all my strength and power will ende=
uour, that I may aunswere the profession and
name of a Christian. And also I will humbly
with all prayers and desires alway craue of al=
mighty God, that he suffer not the seede of hys
doctrine to perishe in my hart as sowen in a drye
* and barren soile, but that he will with the
* diuine dew of hys grace so water & make frute=
full the drynesse and barrennesse of my hart, that
I may bring forth plentifull frutes of godlinesse,
to be bestowed and layed vp in the * barne and
granare of the kingdome of heauen.

Ma. Do so, my childe, and dout not but as thou hast
by * Gods guiding conceaued thys minde and will,
so thou shalt finde and haue the issue and end of this
thy godly studie and eudeuour, such as thou desirest.
and lookest for, that is, most good and happy.

¶The end.

FINIS.

AT LONDON.

Printed by Iohn

Daye dwelling ouer
Alderſgate.

Cum Priuilegio Regiæ Maie-
ſtatis per Decennium.

1570.